Stanley Umezulike

Twisted

First Published in Great Britain in 2019 by
LOVE AFRICA PRESS
103 Reaver House, 12 East Street, Epsom KT17 1HX
www.loveafricapress.com

Text copyright © Stanley Umezulike, 2019

All rights reserved.

No part of this publication may be reproduced, stored or transmitted in any form by any means, electronic, mechanical, photocopying or otherwise, without the prior permission of the publisher, except in the case of brief quotations embodied in reviews.

The right of Stanley Umezulike to be identified as author of this work has been asserted by them in accordance with the Copyright, Design and Patents Act, 1988

This is a work of fiction. Names, places, events and incidents are either the products of the author's imagination or used fictitiously. Any resemblance to actual persons, living or dead, is purely coincidental.

ISBN: 978-1-9163628-0-2
Also available as ebook

ACKNOWLEDGMENT

My deepest gratitude goes to the Almighty God, to Him be all the glory.

This book would not exist without the help of a great team who brought what was once an idea into reality.

I remain grateful to my mentor, Vickie Sanford. Thank you, ma'am, for believing in me and for being a light in my life. I remain forever grateful to my writer friend, Joseph Akogwu for his invaluable input and support at every step of the process. Major thanks to my wonderful friend, Damilola Akinbola who took time out of his busy schedule to edit the first draft of this novel. Dami, I'm blessed to have you as my friend.

To Aoiri Obaigbo, thank you, sir, for your guidance and encouragement. To Richard, thank you for helping me take a bold step in my writing career. To my friends Gbenga and Hanson, Justice and Samuel, thank you for the support you gave to me during my time in the National Youth Service Corps.

I owe a huge debt of gratitude to my brother, Anthony Umezulike. Your kind words kept me going.

To Afoma, Chidimma, Nwabueze, my love and gratitude are boundless.

To Blessing, my number one fan, you are amazing.

To my parents, Mr. & Mrs J.E Umezulike, thank you for positively touching my life.

To my readers, thank you for your support. Your positive feedback brought me joy and a feeling of fulfilment. To my editor, Zee Monodee, thank you for helping me make the story shine. My special thanks go to my publisher, Love Africa Press. Thank you for helping to make this dream come true. To you all, I remain grateful.

DEDICATION

This book is dedicated to my older brother, Anthony Umezulike. Thank you for everything you have done for me.

BLURB

The fate of a family hangs in the balance.

The Obi family live a charmed life, the picture of success and love. But when their only son Emeka marries a woman his parents deem unworthy, the ties that bind begin to unravel.

Wealthy, happy and successful, Emeka's world changes when he sets his eyes on Anita, a beautiful teacher who captures his heart. Though his family disapproves, Emeka is determined to make her his wife. But after what was supposed to be a brief introductory ceremony, his perfect world begins to collapse around him.

Determined to build a happy life with his new bride, Emeka keeps his family at a distance. But he soon finds himself immersed in desperate schemes of his overbearing parents, which gets out of hand when he uncovers a secret that threatens to tear the family apart.

Now, the Obi family members are in danger of losing everything they hold dear. The unimaginable is happening and series of events have already begun to push them into the darkest tunnels of their lives. Will they be able to weather this storm or will they be swept away by the tide?

Twisted

PROLOGUE

50 Years Earlier
Nike, Enugu

The sun was about to set, the insects chirping at the nearby bush. It was supposed to be a cool, calm evening, but the muffled cries of a fifteen-year-old girl destroyed the quietness. Adaobi Okonkwo sat on the ground in a small pathway beside a small bush, tainting the sandy soil with her tears, her once sparkling blue and white school uniform now soiled with dirt.

Adaobi was a young, dark beautiful girl with sharp facial features and eyes once filled with hope and dreams. But now, she felt the world had been so unfair to her. What had started as a memorable experience, a life filled with great promises and joy, had suddenly turned ugly, dreadful, and unforgiving. She touched the slight pooch of her stomach and shivered.

"Three months pregnant!" the doctor had told her.

She found it difficult to concentrate.

My world is turning upside down!

She closed her eyes as a kaleidoscope of memories filled her mind.

"I will not be gentle to anyone who wants to give this missionary school a bad name. This school will no longer tolerate your shameful and immoral acts. You are hereby expelled," Sister Mary, her school principal, had told her.

Her words still echoed at the floor of her mind with its tone of finality. Afterwards, she had gone to meet her high school love, Peter. He had been her last hope.

"Ada, please, I don't want to be seen with you. I don't want to be associated with a girl like you. I have nothing to do with you. I have told you many times, I am not responsible for your pregnancy. This is a big school, I don't know you," Peter had told her with shocking words as he sauntered away with Nkechi, her bitterest rival in school, who was in Peter's arms, giving Adaobi a mocking smile.

Adaobi and Nkechi had been arch-rivals in Grace Memorial Secondary School owned by Reverend Sisters. Both were now in SS3. They were always competing with each other while pretending to be best of friends. At the same age of fifteen, the two girls had both the beauty and the brains. While Nkechi was the President of the Drama Club, Adaobi was the President of the Press Club. In their SS2, both were hostel prefects and always first in inter-school debates and quiz competitions. They dated the cutest guys in school and always sought to out-dress each other.

Adaobi had fallen in love with Peter, the senior prefect, and had gotten pregnant by him after being enticed by his sweet words and promises of living happily-ever-after. It was supposed to be a fairy-tale love story.

But now, the whole thing had turned sour. Nkechi had snatched her boyfriend away from her and had gone as far as exposing her pregnancy to the school authorities. The Principal, a no-nonsense Reverend Sister feared by all the students in the school for her strictness and hot temperament, had quickly expelled her. Her boyfriend had denied knowing her to safeguard his own reputation and position in the school. Peter had wasted no time in flaunting Nkechi as his new heartthrob.

Peter, my love. This is not happening!

Adaobi opened her eyes as tears of shame rolled down her cheeks. Dejection clouded her every moment. Everywhere she turned, she would see shame, embarrassment, and humiliation waiting for her. She couldn't imagine the pain she would put her parents through if they found out.

She placed her fragile hands on her stomach. "I will not bring shame to my family."

Her eyes were puffy and red. Gradually, the sun set, and the colour of her eyes changed to match the resolve she now felt. Something had changed in the young girl. Her eyes were now darker.

She quickly wiped her tears, collected her old school bag, and stood up. She remembered the image of Nkechi in the arms of Peter, giving her a mocking smile.

Nkechi! Nkechi! For all that you have done to me, you will pay! Oh, you will pay dearly!

Her mind remained firm, strengthened by a dangerous determination. She was ready for the inevitable.

Tick tok.

The journey had begun.

CHAPTER ONE

Present Day
Port Harcourt
"Honey, we are late."
"I am coming! Give me five minutes."

Emeka Obi smiled. He knew Anita better than any other person in the world. He could imagine her calmly going through the steps necessary to make herself appear elegant and presentable. That meant waiting for at least another ten minutes, and possibly more, before she was satisfied with her appearance. Women could waste a lot of time getting dressed.

He was not bothered. He would wait. He put on his black jacket and stepped out of the balcony of his two-storey mansion. At the age of thirty, he looked charming and fit; the perfect picture of the most eligible bachelor, his black afro hair neatly combed. Emeka was of average height, dark-complexioned, with flawless facial features. His artfully carved beard gave him an aristocratic appearance.

The early morning Saturday sun shone directly on his face. He walked faster to his car. His gate man, Yusuf, approached him and collected his briefcase to put in the car trunk. Emeka greeted him with a smile, showcasing his perfect set of white teeth.

"Aaaah."

The sound came from a young man in his late twenties, well past average height. Bob yawned as he walked out of the house. The November sun lunged at his face with its furious rays, making him to blink several times. Television weather forecasters were already saying that this year's cold spell would be longer than usual, with lower temperatures. As his master's driver, Bob was always ready to drive him to his destination. He was already dressed up, but sleep still lingered in his eyes. He approached his master.

"Which car are we using today, sir?"

Emeka had high taste for cars, with six vehicles in different corners around the huge compound—a black Cadillac jeep, a white 2015 Range Rover Sport, a Mercedes-Benz Gle SUV, a blue Infiniti Jeep, a red Lamborghini Aventador, and a black IVM innoson-G5 SUV. The whole compound was paved with marble, with a canopy of well-carved flowers situated at the centre to supply fresh air and add to the beauty of the villa.

"Don't worry, Bob. Yusuf has already opened the Cadillac."

Bob nodded and collected the car key from his boss. Emeka smiled. He looked powerfully built in his long, blue Ankara shirt and trousers. As the only child of his middle class parents who had both suffered to raise him up, his life journey had been tough. His father was now a retired secondary school principal, his mother a consultant nurse working in a private clinic at Enugu. She, too, had long retired from the government civil service.

There had been difficult times when his parents had had no money to pay for his school fees. Constant strikes by the labour union shrunk the meagre-pay of their government jobs to almost being insufficient. At one point, when Emeka's school fees in the university skyrocketed, his father had almost given up. Somehow, his mother had managed to pay them so that he could remain in school. Back then, she'd been a senior nurse working at the university teaching hospital at Enugu.

After graduating with a degree in civil engineering from the University of Nigeria, Nsukka, Emeka had worked with a lot of construction companies before opening his own business. His father had proudly helped him to secure a loan from a micro-finance bank.

Now, almost everywhere he looked, he could see the result of his parents' efforts in shaping his life. Emeka had started building a network of connections, welcoming new friendships. With his charming eyes and permanent smile, he was very persuasive and likable. To him, he felt his special gift had more to do with talent than effort.

His major breakthrough came when he secured a government contract to reconstruct the East-West Road. From then, it had been one success after another. At the age of twenty-five, he had begun to deal in import and export of building materials. Later that year, he'd opened his own paint manufacturing company.

Since then, he had been acquiring failing companies. He would buy them and refit them with experts, and before long, they would start generating money. The next thing he did was acquire a big advertising agency. He spent millions in advertising, and he generated even more profit.

Three years later, *Emeka and Sons Group of Companies* finally became a publicly traded company registered on the Nigerian Stock Exchange. Now, it had become a big corporation with shareholders and board of directors, and at the head of this giant sat Emeka, the Chief Executive Officer.

His parents had been worried that he had shunned the idea of marriage. They'd accused him of refusing to marry. For the past seven years, Emeka had focused on his business—from one acquisition to another, from one deal to another. As if he were driving an unstoppable train ... it had to stop temporary when he set his eyes on Anita, who eventually turned out to be the beautiful queen of his heart.

Today, he was travelling to Enugu with his fiancée to introduce her to his parents.

The sound of the horn interrupted his thoughts. He looked up and met her eyes. Anita looked beautiful in her blue Ankara gown. She was a tall, ebony beauty, an inch taller than him. Her eyes were filled with love as she smiled at him.

Emeka approached her, kissed her right hand, and led her to the car. They entered through the back door, and Bob drove the car out of the compound.

Their beautiful mansion was located at Peter Odili Road—a place reserved for the wealthy, part of the Trans Amadi industrial district and a few kilometres away from the Port Harcourt city centre. Port Harcourt, the city that never sleeps, was the capital of the oil-rich Rivers State. Romantics often referred to it as the 'Garden City' because of its flowery avenues and beautiful ornaments.

In less than thirty minutes, they were driving through Rumuola Road, known for its notorious traffic jam. Though still around nine in the morning, the heavy traffic slowed down their journey.

Rivers State government should do something about this hold-up.

Twenty minutes later, they were driving through Aba-Port-Harcourt expressway. They reached Enugu around one in the afternoon.

Located in South-Eastern Nigeria with a population of more than two million, Enugu actually meant 'Hill top,' denoting the city's hilly geography. But yet, Enugu lay at the foot of an escarpment and not a hill. Known as the coal city, it was popular for its cool and serene environment and the coal mineral it had in abundance.

"Are we almost there?" Anita asked anxiously.

Emeka held her hand.

"Yes, get ready. Don't worry, you will be fine. I'm with you," he assured her.

Anita was panicking. A lot of things had been going on in her mind. Today was like a judgment day. *Will they like me? What will they say?*

A lot of questions were flowing through her mind, but only two things helped to calm her down and give her confidence: the love of her life sitting beside her, and the diamond ring on her finger.

She placed her hand with the ring on her chest and muttered silent prayers.

***

Trans-Ekulu, Enugu

"They will soon be here," she said.

"Yes, finally, a woman has captured his heart. I can't wait to see her," he said.

Rita Obi and her husband, Sir Matthew Obi, held hands together as they stepped out of the door of their gorgeous one-storey duplex. Emeka had bought the land at Trans-Ekulu housing estate and built the duplex for them, tastefully furnishing it to their taste. Beautiful trees and shrubs helped to give the compound exactly what they wanted—a quiet, peaceful atmosphere.

Known to her friends as the 'Diamond Butterfly', Rita Obi was a tall, mahogany-skinned woman with an imposing stature and a variable temperament; she could be very gentle and tender one moment, and roaring like a lioness the next. Her husband often joked that not only could she bite ... she could bite very hard.

Because of her imposing physique, a lot of people who knew her now believed that nurses were wicked. But Rita knew she was not wicked. In a man's world, a woman must either keep the men under her feet to gain their respect and admiration, or they would put her under their feet to serve as their tools and properties. She had been eating a lot of food lately, and her curvy, plump frame had made her maids in the house so fearful of her.

Sir Matthew Obi was exactly the opposite of his wife. To maintain balance in a family, there should always be the iron rod and the tender hand. He was the tender hand. A member of the Catholic Knights of St John, he was gentle but firm. Highly conservative and fair-skinned, he was a man of principles and a little above average height, five years older than his wife. At the age of sixty-five, the retired school principal was still ruggedly handsome with flecks of grey hair. He looked up as he heard the sound of a car horn.

"They are here," he said as he smiled.

An elderly gateman opened the gate, and the Cadillac jeep cruised into the compound and stopped in front of the house.

"Stay in the car," Emeka told Bob as he led his fiancée out of the vehicle.

Anita's face beamed as her gown sparkled under the afternoon sun. Emeka maintained a smile on his face as he approached his parents. He had always been very close to his mother—he loved her so much. Since his childhood, her hands had left their marks in virtually every stage of his life. He hugged her tightly.

"Welcome, my son," Rita said as her face lit up in a smile showing her white teeth.

Emeka shook hands with his father. Sir Matthew Obi turned and greeted the young girl.

"Welcome, Nne."

Anita greeted back politely.

Emeka quickly introduced them. "Mama, Papa, this is Anita, the love of my life."

Rita scanned the young woman's face for a long moment, her heavy gaze was intense, making Anita feel uncomfortable.

Quickly, a smile crept back to her face. "Finally. So you are the one. Come and give me a hug."

Anita's discomfort quickly faded, and she became so excited. *What a warm welcome. I can't wait to be a member of this lovely family.* She hugged her future mother-in-law in an earnest embrace, and they entered the house. Soon, they were climbing the tiled stairs. On their way up, she looked down stairs and saw two young teenage girls, probably maids. They were busy hurrying up and down, putting things in order.

At the dining room, expensive plates had already been set on the enormous mahogany round table. They were all served African salad with beef by one of the maids. The second course was pounded yam and vegetable soup with fresh fish, this one carefully served by Emeka's mother.

As Anita observed the way Emeka was enjoying the pounded yam, she made a mental note to add it as one of his favourite foods. The whole family was so adorable. Father and mother sat close to each other as they ate and looked at their only son with eyes filled with love. The son sat facing his parents as he looked at them with eyes filled with devotion. Their faces all beamed with smiles as they cracked small jokes and laughed tenderly.

She was touched by the memorable moment she was witnessing. She wished she had parents like this. Everything was so perfect. Sometimes, the mother would feed the father and help him with a glass of water, and they would all smile. She was looking at a happy family with their golden son at the centre of their universe.

"Nne, which town are you from?" Matthew asked.

Emeka looked on as his fiancée answered. He had already finished eating. His mother was helping him with a bowl of water to wash his hands.

"I am a native of Ikwerre in Rivers State."

"That's wonderful," Matthew exclaimed. "I worked there during my NYSC service year. Some of my friends are from your town. They are all wonderful. Ikwerre people are very welcoming and friendly. They made me feel at home. We are delighted to have you in our midst. You are highly welcome."

Anita blushed. "Thank you, sir."

Before long, they started throwing questions after questions at her, and she kept responding politely.

"When did you meet our son?" This question was asked by Emeka's mother.

Surprised, Anita maintained her smile and answered. "Last year, ma'am."

"Hmmm." Rita looked at her with a renewed interest. "That was when our son was already a ready-made man. When our son was struggling, trying to put his two feet on the ground, no woman wanted anything to do with him."

She paused for a moment, a thoughtful expression was on her face. "Nne, can you say that what attracted you to our son was not his money?"

Anita was overwhelmed by the sudden turn of events. "No, Ma. We met and we fell in love."

There was a crack of laughter.

"Really? That's a unique love story. All in less than a year," Rita said.

Emeka was getting uncomfortable now.

"How long have you been in the city?" Matthew asked.

"I was born and brought up in the city," Anita replied.

"In other words, you grew up in the city ..." Rita left her statement hanging.

"Yes, Ma." Anita was now uncomfortable.

"Hmm. Our son is lucky to have found himself a city girl," Rita muttered quietly. "How many relationships have you been involved in before meeting our son?"

Anita's eyes widened. Emeka quickly wiped the sweat off his forehead and put the handkerchief back inside his pocket. Then, he stopped every other thing he was doing.

Before Anita could answer the question, his mother hurled another question at her.

"Have you known a man before meeting our son?"

"What?" Anita asked in bewilderment.

Emeka's blood boiled with every coming second. His breath had quickened, his mind trying to make sense of the sudden turn of events.

This is madness.

Rita smiled. "Who are you playing pastor's daughter for? Loose it down, young lady. Don't be all innocent on me."

"Enough!" Emeka shouted as he stood up. "What is happening here? This is uncalled for," he said as his parents stared at him, surprised.

"Go to the car. Wait for me. We are leaving now," he whispered in Anita's ear.

"But—"

"Go!"

Anita rose up, fidgeting, and walked slowly out of the house.

"What is this? An interrogation?"

"Don't shout at your mother, Emeka," his father warned.

He glared at his parents and began to walk out of the dining room.

"Emeka!"

His mother's voice always had a way of getting to him. He stopped in his tracks and looked back.

"We have decided," she announced.

"Decided what?" he inquired angrily.

"Emeka, we are your parents. We want what is best for you and our family. You will not marry that girl into this family," his father ordered.

Emeka was highly baffled at his father's words. He had been so happy when he had seen Anita.

Mother!

She had somehow imposed her decisions on father again.

"Anya ya emepego. Her eyes have opened," his mother said. "She is a gold digger."

This was the last straw that broke the camel's back. Emeka turned back and stormed out of the house.

"Darling, I don't understand. What is happening?" Anita asked as he joined her in the car.

"She has done it again, but I won't allow it this time," he said.

"What? Who?"

He ignored her, not in the mood to answer any more questions. "Bob, start this car and drive us out of here."

Bob started the car and drove it towards the exit. The elderly gateman opened the gate, and their car sped off into the hot afternoon sun. What started as a perfect day had turned into a nightmare.

CHAPTER TWO

On their drive home, an unusual silence hung in the car. Anita was so bothered that her fiancé had refused to talk to her. He had kept to himself. He seemed withdrawn, as though in his own world.

Her mind was deeply troubled. Her heart's desire, the greatest thing she wanted, was to marry the love of her life. Now, everything seemed to be in shambles. She could remember how they met, on the day he saved her life ...

"Please come with warm clothing as weather can get wet and cold," said the very bold caveat.

The Obudu Mountain Resort, located at the Obudu Plateau with an altitude of 1,716 metres above sea level, enjoyed a climate typical of temperate regions in the world. The resort had been established as a Cattle Ranch in 1949, located in Obanliku local government area in the northern part of Cross River State.

"Relax, Anita. We are here. Life has been so unfair to us, I know," Aunty Bennet said. She was a dark, fat woman with glasses and a big, cheap black handbag. She had the appearance of a teacher.

Anita had been crying for over a week. She had refused to eat and had kept repeating the same words, "I want to die."

Anita had lived a very difficult life. As the eldest child in the family of four, all the burden fell on her. Her parents were wretched. They could only send her to school with the hope that she would get a job in the future and from there, take care of them and her younger siblings.

Her mother stopped her petty trading after suffering from partial stroke. She had been diabetic for years. When she also began to suffer from hypertension, she became a regular patient at different hospitals. Her fragile health made the whole family live in constant fear of losing her at any moment. Her unending hospital bills caused their father to go bankrupt and be in huge debt, making a lot of enemies in the process.

Anita's father was a road-side mechanic who spent all his money on his wife's hospital bills. He later began to suffer from depression after being frustrated with difficulties he faced in his marital life. Anita always lived with the constant fear that their father would one day leave them all and run away. He was always at bars in the evenings, trying to drink away his sorrows.

Her parents and her three brothers were all staying at Onitsha, surviving with the lowest income. Years back, the family had been residing in Port Harcourt, where she was born. But when life became tough and the standard of living in the oil-rich city became so much higher than they could bear, they relocated to Onitsha.

Anita's mother had begged her sister to allow Anita to stay with her. Thus, she stayed with Aunty Bennet throughout her secondary school education. Bennet was a primary school teacher and an old spinster. She had a good influence on the little girl, and at a young age, Anita began to nurture the dream of becoming a teacher.

When she entered the University of Port Harcourt to study Integrated Science Education, she did a lot of odd jobs just to survive while her aunt managed to pay her school fees. When she graduated, Anita started working as a teacher in a private secondary school.

Her world shattered when she heard the news. Her parents and siblings were all coming back to Ikwerre for a funeral. The person that died was her father's brother, and he had to take his whole family with him in an old Volvo car he had just finished repairing. The accident happened at Aba-Port-Harcourt expressway. The car tumbled and tumbled and eventually caught fire. There were no survivors. In a day, Anita had become an orphan and the only surviving member of her family.

Two weeks ago when Aunty Bennet had told her the news, she'd fainted. The pain was too much for her to bear. As per tradition and custom, they had done the funeral immediately.

Bennet had been worried about Anita's wellbeing. She had met with a doctor who'd told her that Anita might suffer psychological trauma if nothing was done. The doctor had advised Bennet to take the young woman to Obudu Mountain Resort so that she would be able to free her mind from all the tragedies that had befallen her family. If she could be able to see once again the beauty of life, meet new people, and see wonderful places, it might really help her mental wellbeing, the doctor had advised.

After a journey of eight hours, they were finally inside the Obudu Mountain Resort. Anita wiped the tears from her eyes as she looked around in awe and amazement. As they entered the gate, they passed through tall, dense forests where the branches formed a huge canopy that completely shut out the sun.

To her, the big resort was another world entirely. They had lodged at a small hotel and rested for the day. The next day, they visited the dairy section. Her eyes widened when she saw different varieties of cattle bred on the ranch for their fresh milk, butter, meat, and cheese. They passed through numerous waterfalls.

It is so beautiful just looking at the way they sparkled.

On their third day, they were treated with amazing views of rolling mountain ranges. At noon, they rode in a station's cable car. The distance was four and a half kilometres long and may possibly be among the longest in the world. The car ran from the entrance to the resort at the bottom of the mountain, up to the ranch resort at the summit.

It was spectacular. They were treated with the very beautiful views of nature. In the evening, Bennet stayed in the room while she urged Anita to go out and socialize. Anita left the hotel and was amazed when she saw a moving crowd. There were people everywhere, and she quickly followed them.

That evening turned out to be her best yet. The management had a special event organized for them. Tuface and Iyanya, two of Nigerian beloved hip hop artistes, electrified the crowd with their sensational songs.

In the middle of the event, as Anita was sipping from her drink, she saw a well-dressed young man, his hair and beard neatly cut. She couldn't stop looking. As she turned around, their eyes met, and her glass of wine quickly fell on the ground and shattered. She just stood there, stunned.

"Sorry, ma'am. Hope you are not wounded?" the young man asked. He had come closer, with a worried look on his face. She guessed he was older than her.

"No, I'm not. Thanks," she said as her whole body shivered.

Suddenly, there was a commotion as the crowd began to laugh to a joke being cracked by Basket Mouth. When she looked again, he was nowhere to be seen. She left the party afterwards. She didn't understand what was happening to her; she was just thinking about him.

The next day, she was in the mood to swim. She wanted to clear her head. She went to the huge swimming pool, a natural one with its sparkling water and a clear view of the long winding waterfall in front of it. She was wearing a blue swimsuit.

She entered into the water and began to swim. So cold! As she was pushing forward, she looked up ahead and saw a couple with their kids. They were so far away from the pool, but she could clearly observe that they were all happy.

Suddenly, a host of tragic memories of what had lately befallen her family began to invade her mind. She lost her balance and began to sink inside the water. She felt helpless. Her body remained still as it kept descending deep down the huge swimming pool.

She didn't have the energy to fight it. At a point, she couldn't breathe. She gave up hope.

Then, there was a tugging at her feet. A shark? Something was drawing her up, up, up. The hands of someone. They kept pulling her up until she came out of the swimming pool and onto the ground. She felt so weak. The hands were pushing on her chest. Water began to pour out of her mouth and nose. When she opened her eyes, she met those irises she had seen before.

"Are you alright?" he was saying.

"You should have allowed me to die," she heard herself say, and then, she passed out.

***

When she woke up, her eyes met a white ceiling. She abruptly rose up, finding herself on a bed. Surprised, she looked around and discovered she was inside a room.

"Where am I?"

"You are awake."

She turned around and looked at the man standing in front of her. She didn't recognize him at first, but soon, the memories started coming back, and her eyes filled with tears.

"Don't cry, dear. Take this."

He gave her a white handkerchief, which she collected and used to wipe away her tears.

"Thank you for saving my life," she said.

"We should just thank God, my dear. I just happened to be at the right place at the right time," he said with a smile on his face.

He, too, had come to swim that very evening. As he'd reached the pool, he'd been surprised to see her there. They had met before, of that he was sure. Before he knew it, she had lost her balance inside the water. He'd dived in quickly and pulled her up while fighting the water currents.

"I am Emeka. And you are?"

"Anita."

They both stared at each other for a long moment.

"How long have I been here?"

"Since yesterday evening."

"Oh! My aunty must have been so worried."

"Don't worry about that for now, my dear. Yesterday, you said I should have allowed you to die. That was strange."

It was then that she told him her life story. Emeka listened intently. The story was so touching. He told her a little bit about himself. He and his construction company had come to repair the western road at the resort. After getting the job done, he had stayed over for the weekend. That was when he'd met her.

They were inseparable after that, their love for each other so intense, they couldn't bear staying apart even for a day. Aunty Bennet was so surprised when she began to observe that Anita's life had changed. She felt so alive. It was like her niece had come back from the dead.

Anita owed the whole transformation to Emeka. He had saved her life and made it meaningful. Now, she could live for something. She had been living on the edge of life, and he had brought her back. Without him, she would have been lost. She no longer wanted to die—she wanted to live by his side all the rest of her life. He was her world, her everything.

Their relationship moved so fast, like an unstoppable train. On Easter Monday, Emeka had visited her at her one-room apartment. She had been expecting him that day. But she hadn't expected it when he brought out a ring from a small box, knelt down, and said, "Honey, I am not good at this kind of speech. I love you so much that it hurts. I don't know what I can do without you. You are my heartbeat, my breath. The worst thing that will happen to me is if I don't get to spend the rest of my life with you. Please, will you marry me?"

It had been an emotional moment for both of them, with tears in their eyes. This had been her heart's desire to spend the rest of her life with him. That was the only way she could stay sane, and finally, it was happening, right in front of her. Unbearable joy filled her.

"Yes, yes, yes!" she said, and Emeka slid the diamond ring over the third finger of her left hand.

Now remembering it all made her feel so sad. She didn't know what to think. She just hoped that life, fate, or whatever it was, would not take away from her the one thing she desired so much in her life.

Since Emeka had come into her world, everything had been moving on well for her. Her most important dream was about to come true, until suddenly, her worst fears became a reality. She wished she knew what was going on in the mind of her fiancé. She said silent prayers and closed her eyes.

CHAPTER THREE

Emeka's mind was filled with conflicting emotions. *Mother!*

A lot had happened in the past that had made him feel close to his mother. As his mind drifted back into his past, he began to remember the unforgettable moments in his life.

He was six years old. It was his birthday celebration. He was panicking because he believed it would not be his usual birthday event. There was a nationwide strike; he could see it in the eyes of his parents. No money. His parents were always at home. But that afternoon, his mother had organized a surprise celebration for him.

"You are my son. No matter what, I will always do my best to make you happy. I am proud of you," she said to him as she gave him toys, shirts, and lots of gifts. "Now go and play with your friends."

He was so happy that day. Somehow, his mother had been able to do it for him. Maybe she had borrowed, but he was so happy showing off his gifts to his fellow kids with rich parents. He could see envy in their eyes.

He was eleven years old. His class teacher had flogged him in class for coming late even after he had pleaded with her and told her he'd been feeling sick. She had been furious with him and had ordered him to go back home. He had gone straight to the hospital, to his mother's office, and had told her the whole story in tears. His mother had rushed back to the school with him.

"This is wickedness. I can't tolerate this!" she barked in the school headmaster's office.

"Madam, we are sorry. We—" the headmaster was saying.

She had cut him off. "No, you are not sorry. You should be apologizing to my son."

The next day, she registered him in another school, and as a little boy, he was so proud of his mother.

He was fifteen years; he had injured his leg while playing football with his friends. When he returned home, his father scolded him for being so reckless.

"Oh! My son," his mother said immediately after she came back. She had cried with him and treated the wound herself. "Don't worry, my son. You will be a great man in the future."

The young boy spent time with his father occasionally, especially in the evenings, but he spent more time with his mother. He laughed as he listened to her stories, and he did everything she told him. His father had always been there for him—he struggled to pay his school fees at the eleventh hour; he was the one that helped him in securing the loan he used to start-up his business. But Emeka felt drawn to his mother.

As he dwelt on his memories, his thoughts began to focus on the other side of his mother.

He was five years old, playing with a butterfly as his father sat watching, on a Sunday afternoon.

"What are you doing there, Emeka?" his mother shouted immediately after she came back.

The young boy looked at his mother with fear in his eyes. She approached him and stamped her right foot hard on the butterfly, squeezing away any life it had. He had cried so hard that day. His father didn't say anything but just held him, caressing his hair and wiping away his tears.

He was seventeen years old. His first girlfriend, Jennifer, had come to see him. They were chatting happily on the veranda.

"Emeka!"

His mother appeared immediately and sent him to buy a recharge card. As he was coming back, he met Jennifer on the way. She was crying. She ended the relationship quickly, with so much hate in her eyes.

What is happening? Oh, my first love!

"Mum, what you have done?" he had asked her as soon as he entered the house.

His mother had brought a picture and showed him. It was of him and his cousin, Nneka. They were holding hands.

"I told her that you have been cheating on her."

"But Nneka is my cousin. What does she have to do with this? Why are you doing this, Mum?" he asked her in tears.

"I just helped you. I have given her a huge amount of money for her transport fare and warned her never to see you again"

"Mum, you—"

"Don't talk when I'm talking," she interjected. "Don't ever bring any girl into this house again. Focus on your studies and forget about girls for now. You are warned."

It was the worst day of his life.

He was nineteen years old, about to enter the university. "Mum, I want to study Biochemistry," he told her. His father had already agreed.

"You will study no such thing."

Her voice terrified him.

"But Mum—"

"Don't! You will study civil engineering. This discussion has ended."

And he ended up studying civil engineering.

And now, after a lot of pressure from his mother to get married, he had finally found his one true love. At the age of twenty-seven, Anita looked so young, beaming with beauty and intelligence. Fate had brought them together. Nothing could set them apart.

"Emeka! We have decided," his mother had said. *"You will not marry that girl into this family."*

That sounded like what his mother had initiated. Once again, she was against a woman he had chosen. His father had welcomed Anita with so much happiness, announcing he was delighted to see her and saying that some of his friends were from Ikwerre.

In a minute, he accepted her. In the next, he had rejected her. Strange.

Mother!

"Sir," Bob said.

"What?" Emeka asked and looked around, surprised to see that they had arrived at the compound.

It was already late in the evening. His fiancée must have been so worried. He knew her. He knew her very well. He had already made up his mind.

CHAPTER FOUR

Port Harcourt
Anita yawned as she woke up from her sleep. Immediately after she'd come back from school, she had eaten and then had a short rest. It had been three days since they'd returned from Enugu. Nothing was the same. Her fiancé's silence had left her confused.

Now, at mid-Tuesday afternoon, he was not home, the house quiet, until a noise outside woke her from sleep. She stood up and looked through the window. Something was happening in the compound.

Yusuf opened the gate as two big catering trucks came in. One brought in supplies; the second brought in chairs and folding tables. Things began to happen so fast. People she did not know were on the grounds, the chairs being set up for something.

What is happening?

Immediately, she came down the stairs and saw Bob. *My fiancé's driver. What is he doing here at this time of the day?*

"Ma, when is the date for the wedding?" Bob asked.

A wedding?

She wanted to ask whose wedding but thought better of it. Before she could reply, she heard a familiar voice.

"Honey! Can you please come?"

My fiancé is here! Her heart was beating fast. *Oh, God, let this be true.*

She came out of the house and met him and a stranger at the balcony.

Emeka's smile widened when he saw her.

"Honey, I hope you are getting ready for our wedding," he said with a face filled with smiles.

Anita was taken aback by the suddenness of the whole thing. *Am I dreaming?* It felt so unreal.

"Our wedding? Really?"

"Yes, your wedding," the stranger, a huge, dark-skinned woman in her forties, said.

"Honey, meet Juliet. She is a fashion designer, and she will discuss your wedding dress of choice with you."

"I am pleased to meet you, Juliet," Anita said as both she and Juliet shared a brief hug. She then hugged her fiancé, and they shared a passionate kiss.

"Yes, our wedding," Emeka said when they parted their lips. "Are you ready?"

"Yes." Her heart brimmed full of joy.

"I love you, sweetheart," he said.

"I love you, too." She felt so loved. *My fiancé is back*.

Everything was happening so fast. The two women were upstairs in the living room.

"From what I was told, there is no time. Your wedding is this Saturday," Juliet said.

"This Saturday?" Anita asked.

Juliet appeared slightly confused. "Are you surprised?"

"No."

Juliet quickly opened a big fashion magazine with lovely pictures of wedding gowns of different varieties.

"My dear, it is very easy to get overwhelmed when shopping for your wedding gown. No worries. I will guide you through it all. These are their brand names.

We have the A-line which is good for disguising bottom-heavy figures." She pointed to a picture of the wedding dress. "This is the Empire, best for smaller busts or petite figures."

Anita hated it instantly.

"We have the Ball gown." She showed her the picture of the wedding gown—a long, formal dress fitted at the bodice and with a velvet full skirt. "It is a very forgiving style, hiding everything from the midsection, hips, and legs," Juliet explained.

"I like this one." Anita pointed to a picture of a wedding gown with the title 'Mermaid.'

"Oh! The Mermaid. It fits closely to the body from the chest to the knee, then flares out to the ankles. It's best on hourglass figure like yours. Perfect. Your fiancé will love it. It will look lovely on you," Juliet said excitedly.

***

Plans were made, with over one thousand invitations sent out. On Saturday morning, the sun shone bright not just in the city of Port Harcourt, but its brightness also radiated on the face of the lovely couple. Early in the morning, she had been busy with her makeup artists and hairstylists. By ten in the morning, both Emeka and Anita entered inside the white Range Rover Sport, the inscription 'About To Wed' pasted all around the car.

The church was filled to the brim with people in colourful dresses. Emeka had wanted it to be a simple wedding, but because of his status, it had proven difficult. Bennet and Anita's uncles graced the wedding with their presence. Emeka's parents had declined the invitation when informed. Hundreds of people from Emeka's company were all around to witness this great occasion on the glorious day. The first ten pews of the church were filled with the movers and shakers of the Port Harcourt business community.

Emeka was dressed in a black Giorgio Armani suit. As he was standing at the altar waiting for his soon-to-be wife, his best friend, Benson, brought out a white handkerchief and wiped off the sweat forming on Emeka's face. Benson was a tall, dark, and handsome young man dressed in the same black Armani suit, being Emeka's best-man for the wedding. Known as the Port Harcourt big boy, Ben worked with Shell Oil Company.

Suddenly, the crowd looked back as the bride and her bridesmaid began to walk across the aisle. Anita looked so beautiful in her white wedding gown. Her eyes sparkled with love, her face full of smiles. Emeka looked up with pride; he was so happy. *She is definitely worth it.*

When she joined her soon-to-be husband at the altar, the wedding commenced. The man of God, a middle-aged man of average height with glasses, started the service with a series of prayers. The choir sang, the huge crowd watched, the couple held each other's hands, everything was so peaceful.

"We are gathered together on this beautiful day with Anita and Emeka as they exchange vows of their everlasting love," the man of God said.

Both were facing each other, looking each other in the eye.

"As Anita and Emeka take their vows today, we are privileged to witness the joyous love of a new family, a family that will be nurtured and nourished through the devotion of two separate individuals growing together through the common bonds of love.

"The vows you are about to exchange will serve as a verbal representation of non-verbal emotions that are as real as anything than can be seen, heard, or touched. For it is not just the words that you will speak today that will bond you together as one, but the strength of the love and commitment found deep within your soul. At this time, I'll ask you, Emeka and you Anita to join hands."

They each took the other's hands, and the man of God faced Emeka and continued. "Emeka, do you take Anita to be your wedded wife, to live together in marriage? Do you promise to love her, comfort her, honor her, and keep her for better or for worse, for richer or poorer, in sickness and health, and forsaking all others, be faithful only to her, for as long as you shall both live?"

"I do," Emeka said as the crowd watched.

The man of God faced Anita. "Anita, do you take Emeka to be your wedded husband, to live together in marriage? Do you promise to love him, comfort him, honor and keep him for better or worse, for richer or poorer, in sickness and health, and forsaking all others, be faithful only to him, for as long as you shall live?"

"I do," she said with a big grin.

The two diamond rings were brought. The man of God said a short prayer and gave Emeka a ring.

Emeka felt so alive. *This is it.* He remembered when he attended a seminar on marriage life and one of the speakers was speaking on why couples put the ring on the fourth finger of the left hand. According to that person, since ancient times, men believed that a vein called the vein of love ran straight from that finger to the heart, so it became traditional to wear the ring on that finger. The heart is just to the left of the human body, and the fourth finger on the left hand is considered the closest to the heart, the speaker had intoned.

Emeka remembered what his Chinese friend had told him in Beijing. "*Your thumb represents your parents. Your index finger represents your siblings. Your middle finger represents yourself. Your fourth finger represents your life partner. Your little finger represents your children.*"

For him, the ring signified his eternal love for Anita. He brought up Anita's left hand and repeated after the man of God.

"Anita, I give you this ring as a symbol of my love and faithfulness, in the name of the father—" he touched the ring on her thumb, "—and of the son—" he touched the ring on her index finger, "—and of the Holy Spirit—" he touched the ring on her middle finger, "—amen."

He then put the ring on Anita's fourth finger to the huge roaring applause of the crowd.

Anita brought up Emeka's left hand.

"Emeka, I give you this ring as a symbol of my love and faithfulness, in the name of the father, and of the son, and of the Holy Spirit, amen," she said as she put the ring on Emeka's fourth finger to the applause of the crowd.

"You have declared your consent before the church," the man of God intoned. "May the Lord in his goodness strengthen your consent and fill you both with his blessings. I pronounce you husband and wife. What God has joined together, let no man put asunder."

That sealed it.

"You may kiss your bride," the man of God said to Emeka.

"I love you," Emeka said to Anita.

"I love—"

Before she could finish her statement, her husband had already sealed up her mouth in a passionate kiss as the crowd applauded.

Few minutes later, the Range Rover Sport now covered with the inscription 'Just Wedded' drove the newly married couple straight to Hotel Presidential at the heart of the city for the wedding reception.

It was a perfect day for the couple. They came back late in the evening with eyes filled with wedding bliss.

CHAPTER FIVE

Dubai, United Arab Emirates

Dubai, the entertainment capital of the Middle East, was a city of superlatives. For the fastest, biggest, tallest, largest, and highest, the city had it all. With many cultural highlights and all the glamorous modern add-ons, the glitzy city was the United Arab Emirates' vacation hotspot. It had one of the largest immigrant population in the world and was one of the top tourist centres on planet Earth.

With year-round sunshine, intriguing deserts, beautiful beaches, luxurious hotels, huge shopping malls, fascinating heritage attractions, and a thriving business community, Dubai had transformed itself from a desert outpost to a destination *du jour* where millions of people flocked every year for sightseeing attractions, sales bargains, and fun.

When the Boeing 747 aircraft landed at Dubai International Airport in Garhoud district, Emeka and Anita came out hand in hand and collected their bags. Anita was happy. It felt like looking at a sea of people. She had read in one of the airport booklets that this was the world's busiest airport by international passenger traffic.

The couple were dressed in shirts and jeans, their eyes covered with dark sunglasses. They quickly boarded a taxi that took them to Palm Jumeirah Island where they lodged at Hotel Atlantis The Palm at Crescent Road.

It was a Wednesday afternoon. The couple rested for some hours. They had come to spend their one-week honeymoon in Dubai. In the evening, they went down to the restaurant downstairs and ate fresh, delicious sea food.

"How are you doing, dear?" Emeka asked.

They were at the aqua theatre inside the hotel watching a movie titled 'The Notebook.' Anita couldn't believe her eyes. It was like they were inside the sea, with live fishes everywhere. It felt like Heaven.

"Thank you honey, I'm so happy," she said.

"We have not started yet," he said.

***

The next day, they visited the Burj Khalifa. At 829.8 metres, this landmark building in Dubai was one of the tallest buildings in the world. They took the elevators to the observation deck on the hundred-and-twenty-fourth floor.

"This is so amazing," Anita said as they watched the views across the city from the deck. Beautifully designed skyscrapers dotted the city all around, the skyline simply breath-taking.

"Yes, indeed, honey. Dubai is a lovely city. My friends call it the new Paris," Emeka said.

"You have been here before?" she asked when they were back in the elevator.

"Yes, twice."

"Business or pleasure?" she asked as she looked curiously at him with a hint of jealousy in her eyes.

"Business."

Anita felt so relieved, but she did not know why. *What do I expect to hear? It's his past. This is the present;* our *present*, she assured herself.

The next day, they visited the Dubai Creek. It separated the city into two towns with Deira to the north and Bur Dubai to the south. The creek had been an influential element in the city's growth, first attracting settlers here to fish and pearl dive. Small villages grew up alongside the creek as far back as four thousand years ago while the modern era began in 1830s when the Ban Yas tribe settled in the area.

Standing in front of the Dhow Wharfage, the couple watched as cargo were being loaded and unloaded off the dhows. Emeka noticed that most of the dhows have been restored as tourist course boats. They paid a short Arab man who owned one of the cruise boats, and he took them on a leisurely trip across the creek.

It was a beautiful experience. The water appeared blue from far away. They stopped at Deira souks, at the northern bank of the creek where the winding street unfolded the melting pot of the different nationalities that had called Dubai home.

Emeka bought a golden necklace for his wife at the Deira Gold souk. They had a delicious lunch at a restaurant close to the shore where they were served with chargrilled octopus in puttanesca sauce drizzled with a herb-infused butter, dotted with capers and sweet cherry tomatoes.

The couple spent the rest of the week enjoying the gentle breeze of the Jumeirah beach. As they both watched the sun set while sitting on a chair facing the beach, they held hands and laughed. It was a sweet laugh.

"I love you," Anita said.

"Darling, you are the most important person in my life. I am happy that I am enjoying this moment with you," Emeka whispered in her ear and sealed her mouth with a kiss.

When they got back to their suite, there was urgency in their eyes, their bodies burning with need and attention. At this moment, nothing else was more important.

They rushed at each other like they'd been waiting for this moment, and the next was tight hugs and passionate kisses. Emeka dragged his wife to the bed as they struggled to remove each other's clothes. Anita's hands found his shirt, and soon, the buttons scattered on the floor. She quickly attacked his trousers with her hands and groaned when her hand latched onto his hard shaft.

Emeka interrupted her as he swiftly removed her clothes. He let out a gasp when he realized she was naked underneath. She opened her mouth, and he sealed his lips over hers. The kiss was soft and fierce. He went down to her neck, and soon, he was covering her tender skin with soft kisses.

Her husband's body was as hard as a rock, and Anita revelled in excitement as she caressed his back with her fingers. Before she knew what was happening, he had flipped her over and spread her legs wide. She squeezed her eyes shut and gasped when she felt his tongue on her wet valley. He used his tongue and lapped so fast, driving her crazy. Her stomach tightened, and her nipples hardened.

She couldn't wait any longer. "Take me, honey. Take me now."

Emeka replied her with a nod and then pressed his hard rod at the centre of her wet valley. He plunged inside, making her moan and whisper his name. They merged as one and he established a steady rhythm with his thrusts, hitting her at the right spots, sending her to Heaven and back.

A huge wind blew outside, and cold air filled the room painted with the magnificent colour of gold and expensively furnished with the best money could provide. Their shadows reflected on the golden walls. It was wanton and intense. The tempo increased again and became fierce, pounding and demanding, moving faster and deeper until the two shadows became still and the motion stopped.

The two of them lay in each other's arms. Emeka could feel his wife's heartbeat. He caressed her hair tenderly, whispering soothing words in her ear.

Anita closed her eyes, enjoying the moment she didn't want to end.

CHAPTER SIX

Port Harcourt

"Yusuf, open the gate. My husband is already late for his meeting," Anita said to the short, dark gate man.

"Yes, ma," Yusuf said as he quietly rushed to the gate and opened it.

Emeka quickly came out of the house. Bob was already putting his briefcase in his Mercedes SUV. He hugged his wife and kissed her briefly.

"I will miss you, honey," he said.

"Be safe. I will miss you, too," Anita said.

It was Monday morning. They had come back on Sunday, the previous day. Emeka entered the car, and they speed off.

The huge and massive, two-storey building housing the headquarters of *Emeka and Sons Nigeria Limited* was located at Choba. The car entered through the gate. Bob parked it in the garage and quickly opened the door for his boss.

Soon, Emeka was climbing the stairs leading to the conference room, in a hurry. Immediately, he opened the huge metal door of the conference room. Lots of greetings from his top executives ensued.

"Welcome back, sir," Stella, his executive assistant, a tall lady in her early forties, said.

"Thank you, Stella. Hold all incoming calls for me."

He hurried and sat on his black executive chair.

"Good morning, sir," Mark Lang, the Chief Operating Officer—a slim man in his late fifties—said.

Mark was from Jos. Seated beside him was the company's financial officer, Dr. Patricia Babatunde, a dark woman in her late forties. She was tough-looking and rumoured to be very strict, a perfectionist, and it fitted her well. The marketing manager, Mr. Paul Okoro, sat beside Dr. Patricia—he was a middle-aged man from Enugu, in charge of the company's advertising agency. The other three men in the room were the branch managers from Benin, Lagos, and Abuja.

"Thank you all for coming. When did it happen?" Emeka, as the CEO, asked.

"They moved so fast and outbid us," Paul Okoro said.

"It doesn't look good, sir," Mark said.

Emeka caressed his forehead, bothered. They wanted to buy a lucrative cement factory at Benin. Patricia had briefed them before he travelled out that the new addition would bring huge profit to their company. They were still in the bidding process. Now, a Lagos company had outbid them.

"We are going to add another five million. We can't lose," he said.

"Sir, that will amount to a financial strain on our part," Paul Okoro said.

Emeka thought about it and looked at Mark. "How are we faring in the stock market?"

"The Market is volatile, but we are doing fairly well," Mark replied.

"Good. Let's make this deal happen."

For the next six hours, they went through a series of meetings, dealing with problems and making tough decisions. When Emeka got back to his office, a lot of calls and messages were waiting for him. By the time he finished in the evening, he was exhausted. On his way home, he invited his friend Benson over to his house.

***

"Emeka, you look so tired," Benson said.

They were in the dining room. The Port Harcourt big boy was neatly dressed in a white T-shirt and blue jeans, wearing a golden chain on his neck.

Anita brought a tray of food and served it carefully for them.

"Thank you, dear," Benson said to her.

"You are welcome," she said with a smile on her face.

She had served breadfruit. The aroma alone proved mouth-watering.

"This tastes so good," Benson said as they began to eat the food. "How was work?"

"Tiring." Emeka looked at his friend for a moment and asked, "Are you just back from a club?"

Benson smiled. "Yes, you got me."

"Ben, when will you stop?"

"I am just having fun. I am so young. This is the time for me to enjoy life."

"Really, you are not ready to settle down?" Emeka asked with concern on his face. "All those girls you play with, when will you take one home? When you get old?"

"Relax, Emeka. I haven't seen the one," Benson said.

Emeka had known his friend for a long time. He was the ladies' man—handsome, trendy, and enjoyed the attention. At thirty-five, he was older than Emeka and still enjoying his bachelor life, dropping girls like footwear.

Benson was a lucky guy; he worked with Shell Oil Company. The huge pay check gave him the opportunity to purchase a three-bedroom house at Rumuola, the perfect location for a Casanova like him. The girls he preyed on easily fell at his feet, and he didn't want the fun to end.

"Ben, you have to search harder. Your lifestyle is self-destructive."

"Yes, sir. I will. I just need time."

"Time?" Emeka laughed. It was so funny. "At your age, you need time? And you think time will wait for you?"

"You worry yourself too much, Emeka."

They ate in silence for the next five minutes.

"What about your parents? I was surprised they didn't come for the wedding," Benson said.

"Ben, now, let's not go there. I know what you are doing. You are changing the topic."

"And you are avoiding my question."

"They are doing fine. I know my mother. She will call soon."

"Golden boy! The Golden boy! You are so lucky," Benson chanted as he washed his hands. He had finished eating.

Emeka smiled. "You know I hate to be flattered. I am not a boy, I'm a man. And yes, I am lucky. However, it's a bit of hard work, too."

Their conversation lasted for another thirty minutes before Benson said goodnight to his friend and called it a day. It was eight-thirty p.m. when Emeka joined his wife in the living room where she was watching cable news. They spent the rest of the evening together before going to the master bedroom to sleep.

The next day, he came back in the afternoon to have lunch with his wife. She had prepared his favourite, pounded yam and vegetable soup.

"I love this."

"I'm glad you like it."

They were eating in the dining room.

"After this, we are going for shopping," he said.

"Now?" an excited Anita asked.

"Yes, this afternoon. Bob is already waiting for us."

As usual, she took almost twenty minutes to prepare, but Emeka waited patiently. When she came out, they entered the car and were on their way to Heritage Shopping Mall, a huge building at the centre of the city where different assortment of clothes, footwear, and jewelleries were sold.

"All these for me?" Anita asked in awe.

Emeka had bought two pairs of footwear for her, three handbags, and lots of shirts and blouses, gowns, and jeans.

"Yes, my dear. Honey, I just wanted to change your wardrobe. Something that will befit Mrs. Obi," he added with a lovely smile.

Anita's eye widened. "But they are too expensive."

"I have not even started. Order any other clothes that you want."

Anita was so happy. *He is spoiling me. My lovely husband.* She ordered more clothes and jewelleries.

When they came back, the bags they returned home with were so heavy. Bob and Yusuf helped Anita to carry them to her bedroom.

They were happily married. Life was good. As months passed, they began to try to get pregnant. Emeka felt so proud of his wife. He had everything he wanted. Now, something else remained. The one thing that would crown his efforts. He couldn't wait to finally be a father.

CHAPTER SEVEN

It was a lovely Sunday afternoon. Emeka and his wife were spending time together on the balcony of their house. It had been two years since they'd gotten married. The couple had been trying to get pregnant throughout this time with no positive result yet. They were young and healthy, and their love for each other still remained solid.

Suddenly, there was a loud knock at their gate. *Bam! Bam! Bam!*

"Who could that be?" he asked his wife.

"It's Sunday afternoon. I don't know," she said.

Bam! Bam! Bam!

"Yusuf, please open the gate and find out who the person is."

Yusuf, who was resting in his own small house located near the gate, came out of his room with sleepy eyes and sauntered to the gate. Immediately after he opened the lock, the visitor forcefully pushed in the panel and marched inside.

Emeka stood up immediately, surprised.

"Mama! Welcome! Yusuf, take her bag to the guest room."

As Yusuf took her bag, she ambled forward to the house. Nothing had changed in Emeka's mother. Mrs. Rita Obi appeared like someone who had come for a battle.

Anita stood up and extended her hand. "Good afternoon, ma."

"Don't," Rita said as she went inside, leaving the couple confused.

They followed her inside. She sat down on the big sofa in the living room.

"Mama, you must be so tired and hungry," Emeka said. "Anita will prepare food for you."

Rita quickly stood up.

"Let her not dare." She faced the surprised Anita. "Look at you. You married my son for his millions, and yet after many years, you can't even boast of giving him a child."

"Mama!"

"Don't Mama me!" she shouted and continued. "Emeka, when are we going to see our grandchild, eeh?"

"Mama, we have been married for only two years. Why the rush?"

"Only two years!" she cut him off. "You don't even care about your parents again. You have forgotten us. Your father is dying of arthritis, but you don't care. I am the only one taking care of him. At this time that we need you to take care of us, you don't care, all because of this witch," she shouted, pointing accusingly at Anita.

"Mama!"

Anita was already crying.

"Look at her crocodile tears. What did you do to my son? You have tried to turn him against us, but you will not succeed!"

"Mama, enough!" Emeka ordered as he held his wife in his arms. She was now crying on his shoulder. "Don't come to my house and insult my wife. I will not allow that."

Rita was surprised at her son's boldness. Emeka held his hand around Anita's waist as they climbed up the stairs.

Inside their master bedroom, he wiped her tears. He had already told Bob to show his mother to her room downstairs.

Anita furrowed her brow, confusion written on her face.

"She will not try that again. I have warned her. She is my mother, but you are my wife," he assured her.

She nodded and snuggled her head into his chest.

"What about preparing food for her?" she asked.

"She will be fine. Don't prepare any food for her," he said.

"But I have to make an effort so that she will like me."

"Honey, listen to me. You don't have to please my mother. She must not like you. What matters is that I love you, and I will not allow her to treat you bad again."

"I can't believe she called me a witch," Anita said as fresh tears began to drop from her eyes.

"Honey, don't cry. Everything will be fine. She will not call you names again, or I will drive her out of this house."

He wiped her tears and began to kiss her gently. Soon, their need grew urgent, and the kiss deepened. They touched and explored, and he held her in his arms.

The next day, Anita woke up early to prepare breakfast for her husband. She walked down to the kitchen downstairs, but was surprised to see her mother-in-law already there.

"Good morning, ma."

Silence.

Anita walked boldly inside. Her mother-in-law was peeling yam.

"Mama, you can go back to your room. Let me help you," she said.

Rita stopped what she was doing and stood up, looking at Anita with fiery eyes. "How dare you? How dare you order me in my son's house? Whatever charm you are using will not get to me. Look at you. You want to help me. Where are the children? Where are the babies? Why don't you focus on preparing the children for school? Nonsense!"

Anita walked back into the room, crying.

"What is it my dear?" Emeka asked. He had put on his towel, getting ready to take his morning bath.

She told him.

"I told you not to help her. She is an expert in making matters worse."

"I just wanted to prepare food for you," she said in tears.

"Don't worry about me, dear. Just stay away from her."

He pulled her close to him and kissed away her tears. She was in her night gown. He undressed her.

"Would you like to shower with me in the bathroom?"

"Yes," she said.

"Good, let's shower. And forget about my mother as long as she is in this house."

As the cold water poured on her body, Anita's mind was troubled. *How can I forget about her? What can I do to please her? Why will I want to please her? She is already making me feel like I am in a prisoner in my husband's house.*

Her mind was filled with conflicting thoughts. *Oh, God! As long as my husband loves me, I have nothing to worry about.* She closed her eyes and said silent prayers as her husband dried her body with a big towel.

CHAPTER EIGHT

Rumuola, Port Harcourt
"Emeka, when did you start taking alcohol?" Benson asked his friend.

Emeka was sitting down on the couch in Benson's house, looking tired. He had a glass of beer in his hand. His marriage had lasted for three years, and his hopes of having his own children were now looking slim. His mother constantly called him to shout and accuse. Life had suddenly become unfair to him.

"Ben, I am just sad."

Benson looked at his friend. Emeka was beginning to look like a shadow of his former self. *Marriage is terrible.* That was why he didn't want to enter yet. Even he had been worried that Emeka and his wife had not conceived yet. He was deeply concerned.

"Emeka, there is a doctor both of you need to meet."

Emeka stood up and dropped the bottle of Guinness Stout on the ground.

"I'm listening," he said.

"I think it's time for you and your wife to see a doctor friend of mine. He is Doctor Robert. He has his own private hospital at New G.R.A, but is mostly at University of Port Harcourt Teaching Hospital. That's where you will see him."

"Thanks, man. I'm so grateful," Emeka said.

"Everything will be fine. Don't worry. Hakuna matata," Benson said to cheer up his friend.

***

University of Port Harcourt Teaching Hospital, Port Harcourt

On Wednesday morning, the sun was bright, the April weather calm and cool. No rain today, according to the weather forecast. The crowd of people at University of Port Harcourt Teaching Hospital swarmed this morning. Emeka and his wife had been waiting for the doctor for close to one hour.

"You can now go in," said the secretary.

The couple went into the large office. Doctor Robert was a huge, dark, short man, a General Medical Practitioner who treated a wide range of illnesses. He expertly assessed them behind his thick glasses. "Please sit down."

The couple sat down, and Emeka told him their problem.

"About eighty-four percent of couples will conceive in their first year of trying, and those who do not will go on to conceive naturally in their second year," Dr. Robert said and paused. "You said you have been trying for three years and haven't conceived?"

"Yes," Emeka said.

The doctor didn't appear surprised. He had the gait of a professional. "Alright. Do you use birth control?"

"No," both Emeka and Anita said at once.

"Any miscarriage?"

"No," Anita said.

"How old are both of you?"

"I am thirty-three, and my wife is thirty."

"Alright. For you, Emeka, we will do semen analysis. Sperm will be tested for sperm count, sperm motility, sperm morphology, volume, fructose content, and acrosome activity. I will also do a blood test and conduct a hormone test and check for STI. Some STI can cause infertility," the doctor said and scribbled down some information on his writing pad.

Emeka nodded.

"For your wife, we will do a blood test to check ovulation. We will do genetic test, ovarian reserve test, and also check for STI, too."

The couple held each other's hands.

"You both will need to be committed in this. You have just started a difficult journey. You will be fine," he assured them. "Come back tomorrow."

***

Rose Hill Hospital, Port Harcourt

For the next three weeks, Emeka and Anita passed through the different tests, which were expensive and time-consuming.

When the couple came back for the test results on Friday morning, the doctor was not around. His secretary gave them the address of his private clinic.

On their way to the clinic, rain started, a heavy downpour. The sky cried out as dark clouds covered it up. The weather was so bad that Bob had to struggle many times to see clearly. He parked the car in front of the Rose Hill clinic, and Emeka held the umbrella as he and his wife entered the hospital. On reaching the doctor's office, they were quickly ushered in.

"Please sit," Dr. Robert said in his usual professional tone.

They both sat.

"The tests have been done. I must say that I love the commitment both of you are showing during this hard time." He paused and brought out a document. "Emeka, you are healthy. Healthy sperm count. You are fertile. As for Anita, the result showed undetermined infertility."

Her eyes widened.

"What does that mean?" Emeka asked.

"Well, there is definitely a problem, but it's above our range. I will refer you to Dr. Stephen. He is a fertility specialist," he said and brought a card. "Give him this document," he added as he gave Emeka the document and the card and dismissed them.

The couple left the hospital and entered the car.
***

Primetime Specialist Clinic, Port Harcourt

"Bob, we are heading to this address," Emeka said. He gave his driver the card.

Bob collected the card and looked at it. "Number three, Old Aba Road?"

"Yes."

Anita was looking worried. Emeka placed both his hands on her face.

"Honey, look at me." Her eyes met his. "You will be fine. We will be fine."

Primetime Specialist Clinic was a newly built private hospital. Bob parked the car at the garage outside the gate, and the couple stepped out of the vehicle. The rain had subsided. When they entered inside, four couples were sitting, waiting for the doctor. They booked an appointment, paid a thousand Naira, and began to wait.

Anita felt so proud of her husband. *He left his business and everything to help me, to help us.* That was the one thing that had comforted her the most and prevented her from getting depressed.

After waiting for three hours, their turn finally came. They entered the doctor's office and sat down.

Dr. Stephen was a gynaecologist who had additional training in fertility and infertility treatment as a reproductive endocrinologist. A tall, well-dressed man with a thin mouth, he was in his sixties.

He perused the document given to him by Emeka and nodded.

"Do you smoke?" he asked Anita.

It was a shocking question, but he'd asked it with a measured calmness.

"No," she replied.

"How long does your cycle last?"

"Twenty-eight days, sometimes twenty-nine," she said.

He asked her a series of questions, and she answered politely.

"We will do hysterosalpingography," he said.

"What does it mean?" Emeka asked.

"It will be done to evaluate the condition of her uterus and fallopian tubes. X-ray contrast will be injected into her uterus, and an X-ray will be taken to determine if the cavity is normal and ensure the fluid spills out of her fallopian tubes. If there is any blockage, it will be detected," Dr. Stephen explained. "We will also do laparoscopy, and we will do an ultrasound scan to check her ovaries, womb, and fallopian tubes."

"When do we start?" Emeka asked.

"Let her come on Monday. You can come with her if you wish."

"Thank you, Doctor," he said.

"Don't thank me yet."

***

On Monday, Emeka sat down in a chair in the hallway inside the hospital. His wife was undergoing a series of tests. The room where Dr. Stephen was performing the test was white and sterile. Anita was lying down on her back on an operating table.

The doctor did a pelvic exam. Next came an ultrasound. This test used high frequency sound waves to create images of the inside of the human body. Next came the laparoscopy. He administered general anaesthesia into her body and made a tiny incision near her navel. He then inserted a slender viewing instrument called laparoscope. For the next hour, the doctor was busy with the test. When he finally finished, he took the couple to his office.

Anita had a worried expression on her face.

"My dear, don't worry. It's not an ovarian cancer," he said.

"What is the problem, Doctor?" Emeka asked.

"She has endometriosis," the doctor said calmly.

"What is endometriosis?" Anita asked.

"I will tell you," he said, but asked her a series of questions instead, which she provided answers to.

"And you normally have pelvic pain and dysmenorrhoea?"

"Yes."

"Endometriosis is a disease in which tissue that normally grows inside the uterus grows outside it. I detected displaced endometrial growth at the tissue lining her pelvis. Cysts called endometriomas were also detected around her ovaries. They are trapped where they are and need to be removed," the doctor explained.

"Are you talking about surgery?" Emeka asked.

"Yes."

"This surgery, will it affect her ability of getting pregnant?"

"No, it will improve her fertility and increase her chances of becoming pregnant."

"What caused it?" Anita asked.

"The cells lining your abdominal cavity come from embryonic cells. Some of them turned into endometrial tissue, and your immune system was not able to recognize and destroy it. Come back tomorrow for the surgery," the doctor added.

The couple thanked him and left.

The next day, Anita did the surgery, and the endometrial tissue was removed.

"She is okay now. She will get pregnant soon," the doctor assured them when they came back to his office.

Emeka stood up and shook hands with the doctor. "Thank you, Doctor."

"You are welcome."

The couple went back to their house, and as each new day came, their life was filled with new rays of hope.

CHAPTER NINE

Emeka and Sons Headquarters Building, Port Harcourt

The conference room located inside the company's headquarters building was unusually quiet today.

The month of December had come, and Patricia, the company's CFO, had been standing up, droning out the boring end-of-the-year's financial report for hours. Most of the executives were snapping in and out of sleep. It had been a bad year for the company.

"Government is charging us heavily on taxes, and this year alone, we suffered huge losses because most of our businesses are no longer generating enough profit."

"What about our newspaper?" asked Mark, the COO.

"People now prefer checking for news online to buying a newspaper. We may have to sell it to cover our losses."

Emeka's mind was not in the meeting. After five years of marriage, he was beginning to get frustrated. No child yet. His once vibrant life had begun to tear apart, the whole thing adding strain on his marriage. Now, they quarrelled every day, and he was tired of it. All this drama was killing his spirit.

"Sir?" Patricia asked.

Emeka's deep thoughts blew up at once. He looked around the round conference table and noticed that all was not well. He wiped his eyes.

"Go on, Pat," he said.

"Due to the challenges we are facing, we have to lay off some of our workers," she said.

He still held onto a tiny threat of hope. "How about the road contracts?"

River State government had been pouring in billions of money on the Great Port Harcourt city project, and they'd been lobbying for months. Even the governor had assured him of a road contract in the project.

"The road contract will cover our losses," he added.

"Which road contract, sir?" Patricia asked.

Emeka looked at her with a surprised expression.

"The Great Port Harcourt city road contract," Paul, the Marketing Manager, said.

"Oh!" Patricia said. "Sir, we lost the contract to Julius Berger."

"What?" Emeka banged his fists on the table and rose up.

"They were awarded to Julius Berger."

His hands were trembling.

"Paul, how is the advertising agency faring?" Mark asked.

"It's not performing as expected," Paul replied. "We are experiencing bad times in the stock market, too. Our shareholders are beginning to lose faith in us."

Emeka had heard enough. It was already evening. He stormed out of the conference room and quickly walked out of the building.

"Let's go home, Bob," he ordered.

"But Oga—"

"No but. Just drive."

Bob drove him straight home. His head was filled with tension, and the trembling of his hands had not stopped. He was very hungry, and he walked into the dining room.

The moment Anita saw him, she was surprised. His food was not yet ready. It was four p.m. He normally came back by five-thirty.

"You are back," she said.

"Food," he replied as he sat down on his chair in the dining room.

She set the tray of food in front of him. She had made her husband wait five more minutes. He had an angry expression on his face.

"Water."

She filled a glass with water and placed it in front of him.

He brought out the fork and opened the plate of porridge yam. He took a small bite of the yam and suddenly vomited it out.

"What is this?" he barked and stood up in anger.

Anita almost fainted. She hadn't seen this side of him before. He appeared like an angry lion. She was panicking.

"It's porridge yam, sir," she said in shaky voice.

"Really? This food is sour," he said angrily.

"It's not sour. I—"

"When did you prepare it?"

"This morning. I just heated it up now."

He fumed and gave her the fork.

"Come here and taste it," he commanded.

She collected the fork and took a bite. "It's a little bit sour, but it has not spoiled, sir."

"Nonsense!" Emeka's voice roared like thunder. "I will have none of this in my own house," he shouted and walked out of the house.

Anita put her both hands on her head. "Oh, God!"

Bob saw his boss coming. He was sitting on a chair near the balcony. "Where are we going, sir?"

"Bob, you have had a stressful day. Go and sleep it off."

Emeka entered inside the black Innoson IVM-G5 SUV and drove it out of the compound.

***

X Lounge, Port Harcourt

Emeka drove the car straight to Stadium Road and parked the car at the VIP parking garage in front of Port Harcourt X Lounge. Situated right in the heart of city, Port Harcourt X Lounge was a chic, elite lounge and bar. A sleek interior design gave a feel-good vibe that no one could ignore, establishing it as one of the city's best nightclubs.

Emeka was already inside, filling up a glass with red wine. The huge crowd was dancing deep into the night to the song 'Do me' by P-Square. Hot sexy girls in pants and bras were giving the audience their own special captivating dance. He stood transfixed, looking at the contours of their bodies.

Neon lights flooded the huge space. Bodies were humping, grinding, some merged together trying to create some kind of friction while the ones that were already drunk were trying to find their own release. It was a little city of sin, filled with people with troubled minds and hearts that came to release it all in the wonderland.

"Troubles at home?" a soft voice asked.

He was standing close to the bar, now with a bottle of Guinness Stout. He looked behind him, and his gaze met the sexiest eyes he had ever seen. The body these eyes belonged to looked enticing and charming, with sexy curves that offered a lot of sweet promises.

"You got it right on your first guess," he said.

The lady smiled. She was fair and standing just at the right spot where she became a target of the red and blue lights. The strobes flew over her, accentuating her female contours, highlighting her succulent swells. Her tight, tiny dress failed woefully to cover up her body and mask the forbidden valleys.

"You have come to the right place. Why don't you follow me? I promise to offer you a night filled with delight."

Her voice thrummed husky and tempting. Emeka was already drunk.

"Really? Oh, yeah," he said, and she took his hands and led him out of the club. They quickly lodged into a room at the hotel opposite the X Lounge.

That night, Anita waited for her husband, but he never came home. She cried all night.

CHAPTER TEN

The next morning, Emeka came back to his house. When he got out the car, he discovered that his wife was sitting down on the cement floor outside the house, crying, her eyes red and puffy. The December cold was seriously affecting her. Anita was shivering, but not from the cold.

He looked at her for a moment and walked inside the house.

I am not ready for another drama. I am tired of all the nonsense.

His wife followed him inside and stood arms akimbo, facing him.

"You have changed. At first, you were coming back late. I ignored it, but this time, you went too far. I can't believe you are just coming back now," she said in an accusing voice.

"Woman, just leave me alone," he said as he wiped off the red lipstick on his lips.

Anita felt so weak. She had cried out all her tears last night. Anyone looking at her would feel pity for her. The once beautiful young girl full of life looked like a shadow of herself. She had put on weight and now looked older than her husband.

"I won't leave you alone. You can't do this to me." She broke down, sobbing.

Emeka got angry. "What is your problem? Every day, I work hard to provide everything in this house. I have done everything to make you happy. There is nothing you have requested for that I have not provided. But yet, the one thing I ask of you, you have failed to give me."

"I have given you everything. I have devoted my heart, my mind, and my soul to you. What more do you request of me?" she asked.

"A child!" he barked. "Just one child. Is it too much for me to ask?"

"It's not—"

"It's not what? All you know is to complain and nag at me every day. Just leave me alone! I no longer have peace of mind in this house," he said and walked upstairs.

***

"What are you doing to yourself, Emeka? You have changed," Benson said with a hint of astonishment.

It was evening. Emeka had left his house and come to Benson's to clear his mind.

"Ben, I'm tired of people telling me that I have changed."

"Something is killing you inside. What is it, Emeka?"

Emeka told him the problems he was facing in his business and at home. "Seriously, Ben, I don't know what to think. I'm afraid I will go over the edge. And my wife is making things worse."

"Please, take it easy with your wife. Both of you need to stay strong. Look at the way she looks now. Just take it easy with her."

Emeka held his hand on his face and took a deep breath. *This can't be happening.*

He closed his eyes and remembered the good times, when life was good, business was good, and Anita was lovely and amazing. She had gone through a lot just to be with him, and he had sacrificed so much just to make her happy. He felt like fate had given him one big blow. He had been drinking too much, and he didn't like it.

I will make it up with my wife. We will open a new page.

He stood up, thanked Ben, and drove straight home.

CHAPTER ELEVEN

For the next two weeks, things worsened between the couple. The quarrels increased, and Emeka began to hate the idea of coming back home. Sometimes, he went to nightclubs and didn't come back at night.

Anita felt she was the reason for the problems in her marriage. She would do everything to perfection, all to please her husband, but he ended up despising her. Now, she cooked food on time; she did everything right to make him happy, but to no avail. The Christmas season that year was her worst. There were no gifts, no hugs, no good wishes—her husband's love for her was fading fast. She could see it in his eyes.

On a Monday morning on the second week of January, no sun shone, the cold unbearable. Emeka was sitting down in his office, but his mind was far away. A lot of reports he had to attend to lay on his table, but he couldn't concentrate. He was praying that time would stand still so that he wouldn't have to get back home. He was tired.

"Sir."

He didn't hear it. He couldn't hear it.

"Sir ..."

This time, the words snapped him out of his deep thoughts.

"Sorry, Stella." He looked at his executive assistant and collected the envelope she handed out to him.

"Is anything wrong, sir?"

"No, no, no. Everything is alright. What is this?"

"It's a document brought by the marketing manager. Please sign after going through it."

Emeka opened the envelope, brought out the document, and read through it. He took out his pen and signed.

"Approved," he said and gave the document back to Stella.

"Thank you, sir."

He nodded and waved her off.

To his greatest dismay, time moved so fast. By five, he was tired. He picked up his jacket and got ready to go home. In the next five minutes, he found himself back in his car on his way home.

The moment he had reached home and entered his room, there was a huge noise outside.

Bam! Bam! Bam! Bam!

"Who is it this time?"

He came down the stairs and quickly went out of the house. That was when he saw Yusuf opening the door for two women.

"Mother!" he said, surprised.

"Let's move," his mother said, dragging the hand of a young girl carrying a small bag. She pushed the girl forward.

"Where is she?" she shouted. "You will not kill my son. I will not allow it."

As the whole drama was unfolding, Anita opened the door and came out. Emeka stood rooted to the ground.

Things happened so fast in the next four minutes. Rita went inside the house and brought out Anita's bags and ordered Yusuf to take them outside the gate.

Anita broke into tears as she looked at her husband for help. "Honey! Darling, please. This is not happening! Remember our vows."

But Emeka stood motionless on the ground, looking like an ordinary spectator.

"Yes, this is happening," Rita said. "You have done your worst. You have destroyed our family and kept my son in bondage. You are no longer needed in this family. Go away, and leave my son alone!" she shouted as she pushed Anita out of the gate.

She approached her son and hugged him. "Emeka, oh! Look at what she has done to you. Don't worry, the worst is over. Amaka, come here," she called.

The young girl she came with approached her and stood by her side.

"Amaka, this is Emeka, my son. Emeka, this is Amaka Okafor. I brought her all the way from the village. She will be here to take good care of you," she said and led the young girl into the house.

Emeka stood still, with no show of emotions on his face. After a few minutes, he staggered back into his house like a man whom Fate had given more than enough drink of pain to swallow. He was like a man who had suddenly became powerless to stop the fire that had started to engulf his house.

CHAPTER TWELVE

Amaka Okafor did not have the image of a typical village girl. Instead of appearing shy and dull, she was dark, tall, and slim—an ebony beauty in its perfection. Her long eye lashes were smooth and black. Her deep, captivating smile never failed to show the dimples in her flawless face. Her red, generous lips made her look like a vestal virgin, with the power to make all of a man's problems go away. She had the waist of a dancer and the slender legs that naturally complemented it.

She was born without a silver spoon in her mouth, but yet, she had been desired by every man that came her way. At the age of twenty-four, she was young, fresh, and simply irresistible. She came from a family of four children. Her elder brother and two elder sisters had all married. As the last child, she was the pride of her parents, poor farmers who struggled every day to put food on the table. They had always seen Amaka as the miracle that would change their condition.

Both Amaka's family and the Obi family all hailed from the same small town of Emene in Enugu State. That was how Emeka's parents got to know Amaka. They were good neighbours. She always fetched water for them whenever they were back in the village. The young girl was gentle and kind. Mrs. Rita Obi had long observed that Amaka was never tired of working. She saw in her the perfect choice. She had discussed her plans with her husband, who'd agreed.

When they told Amaka's parents, they believed that the miracle they had been waiting for had finally happened. Their daughter was going to marry into a rich family. Who would reject such a gift from God?

After the necessary cultural arrangements were made, Emeka's parents took the young girl back to Enugu. For the past six months, she had been taking care of Emeka's father. The old man was now seventy years of age, using a wheelchair due to his severe arthritis.

The next thing for Mrs. Rita Obi to do was the most difficult in her plan. To drive Emeka's wife away and properly introduce Amaka to her son and put her where she belonged.

She was surprised when her son didn't put up a fight. The whole thing confirmed her fears.

That witch almost killed my son. I am lucky that I came just in time.

That Tuesday morning, she went downstairs and discovered Amaka already cooking food in the kitchen. She smiled.

"Good morning, ma," Amaka greeted.

"Morning, Nne. I hope you slept well."

"Yes, ma."

"Good. You are already cooking one of his favourites. He will come down by seven-thirty to eat. Take good care of him. He will love you. Your delicious foods will do part of the work for you, and with time, you will work your way into his heart."

As she was advising her, Emeka walked past them, fully dressed.

"Oh! My son. You are already going to work. Aren't you forgetting something?"

Emeka stared at his mother for a moment.

"Good morning, sir," Amaka greeted him.

He didn't reply her.

"I'm not forgetting anything, Mother. Now if you both will excuse me, I'm already late for a meeting," he said and walked out of the house.

Rita was surprised. One minute, she thought she understood her son. The next, she was lost of words.

She looked at Amaka. "Don't worry, Nne. He will come around. It will only take just a little time."

***

She was on the run; someone was chasing her. A tall figure, but she was unable to see the face. The figure's footsteps came closer now. She dashed through a tiny track in the middle of a forest. *I just have to make it to the stream, and then, I will be out of his reach.*

She ran as fast as her legs could carry her. But before she could reach the stream, she hit her foot on a big stone and fell. The figure was hovering above her now. It brought out a knife, raised it up, and was about to bring it down on her chest. She screamed so hard ...

Rita woke up in the middle of the night, panting. She was in her son's big house and prayed she hadn't woken anybody up.

Did I scream?

She had been having this nightmare for the past fifteen years. It always stopped where the figure wanted to kill her, and she would wake up and lay awake for the rest of the night.

She sat on her bed and tried to calm herself down. She closed her eyes, opened them, then closed them again. The memories of her past started to flood her mind.

She panicked and opened her eyes once more. She looked tired and tormented. Her head was hot. She'd began to notice that she was constantly having headaches along with pain in her abdomen. And after a while, it would cease only to resume again. She made a mental note to visit the hospital. The pain stopped, and she was once more surrounded by her dark memories.

I could never forgive myself. She was shaking her head. *They must never find out, but if they eventually find out, I hope they will forgive me.*

CHAPTER THIRTEEN

Choba, Port Harcourt

Tears filled Anita's eyes as she sat down at Choba Junction and cried silently. Angry voices, frayed nerves, accusations, and counter-accusations had damaged her once lovely marriage. She had never believed that her husband would give up on them.

She had slept outside the house that evening, and in the morning, she had been going round the city looking for a place to stay. Port Harcourt was no longer the cool place it used to be. Violence in the Garden City had gone full circle. Sad tales of death, kidnappings, armed robberies, and cult clashes had turned some parts of the city into a jungle. She had thanked her God when she'd woken up in the morning unscathed.

Emeka has forgotten our vows!
For better or for worse.

She closed her eyes as she remembered them. She couldn't believe that her husband had chosen his mother over her. When she remembered that she had no one, it pained her so much. She felt as if her heart had been ripped apart.

She stood up and entered a cab.

"Where to?" asked the driver.

"Elelenwo," she said.

The driver put her three bags in the trunk of his car, and in the next two minutes, he was driving straight to Elelenwo.

Times had changed, and the oil-rich city has changed with it. With growth and opportunities, the population of the Garden City had swelled. The increase in population fuelled a property boom that had opened up and linked the major enclaves of the city that now extended from Emohuo, headquarters of the local council, through Choba into Rumuokuta, stretching into Okrika. The blessings of its status as a fast-growing cosmopolitan city had equally come with the headache of knotty traffic jams that sometimes stretched for several miles and spanned for hours.

On their drive to Elelenwo, huge traffic jams derailed them, some of the junctions locked up, and the driver had to take another route. Anita sat on the back seat, her eyes filled with sadness. She was heading to her late Aunty Bennet's place.

Two years earlier, news of her death had almost torn her heart apart. She had lost the rest of her family in a car accident and couldn't bear the pain of losing her aunt to breast cancer. It was Emeka who was able to console her and clean away her tears. Now, he had bowed down to his mother's pressures and turned his back on her.

I have no one! No one. Fresh tears began to drop from her eyes.

***

Elelenwo neighbourhood consisted largely of mixed-income apartments. Public and privately owned estates gave the neighbourhood a peaceful look. Low-rise shops and recharge card centres dotted the sidewalks.

"Stop me at number thirteen," she said.

The driver drove for few minutes and finally stopped the car in front of a one-storey building. Anita still remembered that her late aunt used to live here.

She entered the compound, dropped her bags close to the gate, and walked up the stairs. She stopped in front of her late aunt's room and knocked.

In a minute's time, the door slowly opened, revealing a fat woman.

A stranger! Anita was surprised.

"I am looking for Aunty Bennet's younger sister, Ifeoma. She is supposed to be staying here."

The woman looked at her with a confused expression. "I have never heard of that name before, miss. I and my husband have been staying here since last year when we rented it. Please, if you will excuse me, I am cooking," she said and shut the door.

A small sound made Anita to realize that she was bolting the door from inside. Feeling so tired, she staggered down the stairs. She collected her bags and took a cab to Rumuomasi.

I don't know if she will be around.

When the driver stopped her at Rumuomasi, she collected her bags and trekked down the street. At still ten in the morning, girls in their thirties with mini-skirts flooded the joints in the area.

Anita stopped in front of an old brick building. It was a public yard, most of its occupants single ladies. She entered and stopped in front of a door at the end of the apartment building.

When she knocked, a fair, plump lady with heavy makeup opened the door. She had bony eyes. Some parts of her skin were light while others were dark. Without doubt, she appeared to be among the dark ladies punishing their skin, bleaching it with cheap body creams, all in an effort to become something else.

"Oh my God! Anita," she shouted and hugged her.

"Chimdi, thank God you are around," Anita said as tears dropped from her eyes.

Both girls had been friends since their secondary school days. Life happened, and each had followed a separate path. Chimdi looked at her friend and knew that all was not well.

"Please come in."

Anita entered the one-room apartment and dropped her bags on the carpeted floor. The room was scantily furnished. Lots of creams and makeup boxes littered across the room. A big mirror hung in the centre of the room.

For the next twenty minutes, she told her friend all that had happened to her.

"My dear, men are pigs. I use to tell you, but you didn't want to listen," Chimdi said as she comforted her. "They are all the same. Your husband is a shameless man. Oh! He chose his mother over you. He has no bone. Men are so weak. That's why I can't commit to any man. Stop crying, my dear. You will be fine. May God punish all of them."

***

Emeka was in his room feeling so tired. He had just finished taking his bath after a long, busy day. His mother was still staying in the house. She had been here for the past week.

Is it that she doesn't want to go?

The thought of the two women staying in his house constantly annoyed him. He had observed that they were always having whispered conservations.

Whatever they are plotting, it will never work. As he lay back on his bed, he heard a knock on his door and jerked up suddenly.

Who would that be?

He was wrapped in only his big towel. He stood up and walked closely to his door and opened it.

"Good evening, sir," Amaka said.

He looked at her and grew very angry.

"And what are you doing here? My mother sent you?"

"No, sir. I came so that we can spend time together."

Emeka pushed her backwards.

"I don't need you. Please don't disturb me again. If you are lonely, go and spend time with my mother," he said and closed the door.

"Nonsense!" he muttered under his breath.

CHAPTER FOURTEEN

Emeka and Sons Headquarters, Port Harcourt

"Stella, you can call him in," Emeka said. It was a bright Wednesday morning, and he had just entered his office.

"Yes, sir."

The door opened, and Mark Lang, the company's COO, entered the office.

"'Morning, Mark. It's so nice to see you," Emeka said as both men shook hands. "You can sit."

The slim man sat down on the soft leather chair across the huge mahogany desk, facing his CEO.

"You booked an appointment to see me ..." Emeka left the statement hanging in the air.

"Yes, I did. There is some form of activity going on in the company, and I felt I owe it as an obligation to come and advise you as a friend."

Emeka sat up, highly focused. "Some form of activity?"

"Yes," Mark said. "The company had been suffering heavy losses for the past five months. We have been losing major contracts. Some of our small businesses are not performing as they should. We are doing badly in the stock market, and because of this, our shareholders and our customers are beginning to lose faith in us. Now, the board wants to intervene."

"Intervene? Without my consent?"

"Can I be frank, sir?" Mark asked.

"By all means."

"The company is suffering recently under your leadership. So the board wants to do a shake up."

"A shake up? I was the one that built up this company from nothing and without help from anybody. I am doing my best to put things in order."

"Sir, yes, you have fifty percent of the stock, but now that we have gone public, we are loyal to our customers and shareholders. Personal interest aside, of course. This is a standard organization, and you know what happens next. The board will call for an emergency session, and if the result of their vote shows they have lost confidence in you as the CEO, you will have to step down, and the board will vote in a new CEO."

Emeka remained silent for a long moment. He didn't talk.

"I just wanted to let you know, sir," Mark said as he stood up and left the office.

Throughout the rest of the day, Emeka lost concentration in his duties, his mind deeply troubled. When evening came and Bob drove him home, he lifted his hand and said, "Thank you, Bob. Don't worry about me. I will just go and clear my head."

Bob came out of the car, and Emeka went to the driver's seat and sped off.

***

Amaka was in her room in the house waiting for Emeka. It was very late in the evening. Her soon-to-be-mother-in-law had bidden her goodnight and was already asleep in her room. She was worried that he had not come back yet. She had already prepared his food and had set it for him in the dining room.

For over two weeks that she had been in the house, Emeka had always been harsh to her.

What did I do to make him hate me?

She had done everything to impress him, but he had always kept rejecting her. She had his parents' support, but still, she was beginning to feel unwanted in the house.

She looked at the time—ten p.m. Suddenly, she heard a car horn, and a little while later, the sound of a car driving into the compound. She went down the stairs, surprised to see Emeka staggering into the house. Her eyes widened; he was drunk.

I have to help him through the stairs so that he will not fall.

She helped him climb the stairs with great effort. His breath smelled of alcohol. When she led him to his room, she turned to go, but strong hands held her back. Under the influence of alcohol, Emeka's eyes were filled with lust and desire. He pushed her roughly inside the room, and she fell on top of the big king-size bed.

Amaka began to panic as Emeka removed the rest of his clothes. He placed his hands on her dress and tore it open. Some of the buttons fell on the marbled floor. She was breathing fast. In few minutes, he pushed in through her virginal entrance.

She closed her eyes as tears dropped down. The pain was excruciating. The blood spurted out and stained the sheets as he plunged in with deadly assault.

It will end soon, she comforted herself as she began a countdown.

The thrusts and pounding became fast and furious, and after two minutes, Emeka released his troubles and deep tensions inside her and collapsed back on the bed, well-spent.

Amaka quickly climbed out of the bed. She was feeling pains around her waist. In the next five minutes, she was in the bathroom crying as the small rain of water began to wash away the blood.

Will tomorrow set everything right and make my man finally accept me, or will it bring forth bad tidings?

CHAPTER FIFTEEN

Early that Friday morning, the sun was about to break through the horizon. Mrs. Rita Obi was watering the flowers in her son's compound. It had been four weeks since she first came with Amaka. The servants in the house had requested to help her, but she had refused. She wanted to water the flowers herself.

Suddenly, she heard an unusual sound.

She stopped and listened.

Someone is vomiting!

She crept closely to where the sound was coming from, surprised when she saw Amaka coughing and vomiting.

"Amaka!" Her eyes widened.

She wanted to ask what was happening to her but put her hands on her mouth as another thought entered her mind.

"Morning, mama. I don't know what is happening to me," Amaka said. She was still in her nightgown, afraid her soon-to-be-mother-in-law would shout at her.

"Don't worry, my dear. It may be a small headache. Get dressed. By eight, we will be going to a clinic. You will be fine," Rita assured her.

"Thank you, ma."

She told her son that Amaka was feeling sick, and he ordered Bob to drive them to the clinic.

By eight-thirty a.m., they were inside a small clinic at Trans Amadi. Rita had already told the nurses what she wanted them to do.

"Mama, they are not giving me any drug for malaria. They said they are going to conduct a test."

Rita kept quiet as she looked at Amaka with a thoughtful expression on her face. Finally, she said, "They are going to carry out a pregnancy test."

Amaka looked down immediately.

"How do you know?" she asked, feeling very shy.

"You forget that I am a nurse. I know the signs. You will be fine."

The test was done, and in ten minutes, one of the nurses came out with the result.

"And?" Rita asked as she looked up.

"Positive. She's pregnant," the nurse replied.

Rita smiled as her face sparkled up.

"My daughter, you have made my day. Tell me what happened again."

Amaka told her what happened that night as she listened intently.

***

"Mama, I can't believe what I'm hearing. I'm not responsible for her pregnancy. She should go and find whoever is responsible."

It was late evening, and Rita had given her son what she called the good news but had been surprised at his reaction. Amaka was sitting beside her in the living room, crying.

"Shut up, Emeka. You are the one, and you know it. You are the only man she has ever been with, and you know it."

"Both of you, your plans will never work," he fired back.

"Emeka!" His mother's voice made him to stop. "How dare you talk to me like that? I carried you in my womb for nine months. I have always been by your side seeking your interest. You must treat me with respect, and you must respect the mother of your unborn child." Her voice carried authority.

Emeka didn't say any word again. The next day, his mother went back to Enugu.

As weeks became months, Amaka began to feel frustrated in the house. She thought the whole rejection would end now that she was pregnant for him. She thought he would finally accept her now that she was carrying his child, but she was wrong.

"You are not mine. I can't take what I didn't fight for. I can't accept what was dropped freely on my lap. This is too good to be true. This is one of my mother's games, and I am tired of all the drama. I am sorry that you are caught in the middle of all this. She is using you. I can't accept what is not mine. It goes against everything I believe in," Emeka had told her bluntly in the fifth month of her pregnancy. She had come to his room late in the evening, and he had pushed her away.

Amaka spent long, lonely nights on her bed crying while carrying the unborn child of a man that had rejected her.

"Are you too dumb to understand it? I don't love you. You can't have me. You don't belong to me, and my position on this will never change."

"We can get to love each other. Let us first get to know each other."

"That's impossible. We can't get to know each other. Just leave me alone."

"But I am carrying your child. Your unborn child!"

"Oh! My child? You think you can tie me down with this pregnancy?"

Amaka felt pains in her heart. The man she so much desired hated her with as much fervour. He had been harsh to her. She felt unwanted in his house.

***

The contractions started during the ninth month of her pregnancy. Emeka was not around that day. Bob took her to Rose Hill Clinic, and Dr. Robert attended to her. When Emeka came to the hospital that Thursday morning, he was ushered into the doctor's office.

Dr. Robert wasted no time. "Congratulations, Emeka. You are the father of a bouncing baby boy."

Emeka was surprised. "Really, Doctor, how is she doing?"

"Both the baby and the mother are safe. They are doing well."

A baby boy! An heir! he thought as he followed the doctor to the recovery room to see them.

At the recovery room, Amaka looked up, not sure of what Emeka's reaction would be as she noticed his presence in the room. She was wrapping the baby in her hands.

Emeka looked into the innocent eyes of the baby and almost cried. *He has my eyes.* As he held the baby in his hands, he thought, *Oh God, what will I do?*

CHAPTER SIXTEEN

"Mama, I don't understand the reason for this celebration," Emeka said, annoyed.

He had told Bob to inform his mother that the girl she'd brought to his house had finally given birth, and his mother had come back to Port Harcourt the next day. She had prepared a delicious meal for them and had called for the whole family to celebrate. They were at the dining room, Amaka sitting near his mother. The baby was finally sleeping in her room after Rita had spent hours with him.

Rita dipped her fork into a big piece of fried chicken and said with food in her mouth, "A bouncing baby boy! I can't believe I am now a grandmother. Emeka, I am so happy. We have to thank God for safe delivery."

"But Mama—"

"What is wrong with you, Emeka? You have changed. How is your business doing?"

"Mama, don't change the subject."

"Then let's celebrate in silence. Just enjoy the food."

As they were eating and drinking, Rita smiled widely. *Mission accomplished!* she said in her mind. But as she continued to eat her own food, the headache and the pain in her abdomen returned with astonishing fierceness and she panicked.

Suddenly, her stomach grumbled and she excused herself to go to the restroom. She'd developed frequent bowel movements. All these had become a regular occurrence. She wondered what was happening to her.

***

Trans-Ekulu, Enugu

"A son!"

"Yes, a son. A baby boy!"

"That's a special gift from God. Mat, I am so happy for your family."

At the same time the rest of his family were celebrating in Port Harcourt, Sir Matthew Obi was in his compound in Enugu relaxing on his wheelchair with his long-time friend Patrick under the gentle afternoon breeze.

They had been friends for over forty years. At sixty-nine, Patrick was just a year younger than his friend. He was tall and big, a figure befitting a judge of Enugu State High Court. Patrick's long legal career was far from over. He was dark with small wrinkles on his face, his eyes hiding themselves behind big eye glasses.

Now both friends were heading slowly into old age. While Mat suffered from arthritis, Patrick was diabetic. A man that preferred keeping to himself, Patrick had been divorced for more than thirty years, his marriage having lasted only a year. With no child of his own and no interest to marry again, the legal giant had focused his whole attention on his career.

"I am so proud of that young lady. She has been so good to me and my wife," Mat said.

"Her name is Amaka, right?" Patrick asked.

"Yes, so young and lovely."

Patrick smiled as he kept quiet for a long moment. "Mat, you know your son had wedded in the church before. I don't know if he can wed again for the second time with another woman. I am thinking of something else."

"Okay, go on."

"They are free to come to my court and do a court wedding. It's more official. I will give them all the help they need."

Matthew smiled. "Thank you, Pat. You have been of immense help to my family. We are in your debt."

"Don't mention. You would do the same for me."

The two friends laughed. Mat ordered drinks, and his servants brought two bottles of small stout and dry gin. It had already made their stomachs big. Both of them knew that what they were doing was against doctor's orders, but they continued to gulp down the drinks in a happy mood.

Matthew smiled as another thought entered his mind. *No going back. I did what I had to do.*

CHAPTER SEVENTEEN

Port Harcourt
The season was wet and windy. Every day seemed to give birth to another heavy rain. Emeka lay on his bed, struggling to sleep. The previous day, his mother had gone back to Enugu after celebrating with them. That Friday evening, he'd gone to bed early. He had been struggling to sleep ever since. The roar of thunder made him sit on his bed. He brought out his watch and checked the time. Six a.m.

Shit!

Saturday morning!

Suddenly, he heard a deafening cry.

What is that?

He ran out of his room like a man being chased by his enemies. He kept approaching closer to the source of the sound.

Amaka's room?

A thoughtful expression crossed his face. *Why can't this girl leave me alone?*

When he stopped in front of the door, he opened it without knocking and entered inside.

The room lay in chaos. He didn't see the baby. Amaka was crawling on the floor, crying out her tears.

"Amaka!" he shouted. "Why are you determined to disturb the peace in this house? This is still early morning; what is wrong with you? I can't sleep peacefully in my house again—"

He stopped his grumbling and began to understand why he wasn't able to sleep all night. The noise from this room had been disturbing him.

Chineke mee!

"You have been crying all night?"

Amaka stared at him, her hair scattered. She had been crawling on the floor.

"The baby," she managed to say.

"And what about the baby?" he asked.

"The baby is dead!"

"What!"

Shock froze him. He rested his body against the wall and began to think about the implication of what he had just heard.

"When did this happen?"

"In the middle of the night."

"This can't be!" he shouted. "No!"

He was shaking his head.

Suddenly, another thought entered his mind, and the expression on his face changed.

"Oh! You killed your baby at night so that you will put it on my head."

"No ..." Amaka responded as she stood up.

"You set me up and thought you will tie me down with your pregnancy. I know what you and my mother did," he said as he pointed an accusing finger at her.

"I—" Amaka opened her mouth.

"Now the baby is dead. And you will not bury the baby in my compound," he shouted and stormed out of the room. "Bob!"

No answer.

"Bob!"

"Sir," Bob responded and came swiftly to his master's side.

"Collect this woman's bags and belongings and throw them out of my house," he ordered.

Emeka's eyes were red with anger. He faced the trembling Amaka and said, "You are no longer allowed to stay in my house. You must carry your dead child and leave at once. Do you understand?"

"Yes," Amaka said in a trembling voice.

In the next ten minutes, Bob helped her to pack her two bags. *I pity this woman. I don't know what is happening to my Oga.*

He led her out of the compound and gave her a thousand naira.

"Thank you, Bob. I can't thank you enough," Amaka said in tears.

She carried her bags and her dead baby and disappeared into the heavy mist of the morning dew.

CHAPTER EIGHTEEN

The next day, Emeka was sitting on the balcony of his house. That Sunday evening, he was restless, a lot of things on his mind. Sometimes, he would try to fight back tears. He felt so lonely and angry. His friend Benson had travelled to Abuja. He was facing problems at home and at work.

He stood up and collected the key of his blue Infiniti jeep from Bob. *I need peace of mind.* He was beginning to lose hope on everything. He took the car out of his house and drove around Trans Amadi, still bored and restless. Nothing interested him again.

He drove the car back to his house. As he came out of the vehicle, he was surprised at the person he saw. "Mother!"

Rita Obi was dressed in a white blouse and black trousers, her eyes snapping up and down.

"Emeka, have you gone mad?" she asked in anger.

"Mama, let's go inside," he said.

"Don't order me," she said as she raised her hand. "Amaka called me and told me all that happened. I don't even know exactly where she is right now. She doesn't know anyone in this city, and you chased her away just like that? Where do you want her to go? I can't believe that you have stooped so low to the level of being a murderer."

He was taken aback by his mother's stinging words.

"Mama!" he cried out as his eyebrows widened.

"Don't you dare shout at me! You chased her away after you succeeded in killing the baby. Your own son! You removed the one thing that will connect her to you and got rid of her—"

"I did not kill the child!" He cut his mother off.

"Yes, you did, you ungrateful ingrate! After all that we have done to raise you and make you what you are today, this is your thank you note to us. You are—"

"Enough, Mother!" He had heard enough. His eyes were blazing. "Enough of all this! I am tired of all your games and manipulations. All through my life, you have always been controlling my life for your own selfish interests. My business is stormy right now. At work and at home, everything has turned upside-down. I am losing my peace of mind all because of you and your wicked plans. You rejected the woman I love and drove her out of my house. You set me up with a village girl, and now, you accuse me of killing her child.

"It is always about what you want and what you need, but all that ends right now. Now that I think of it, I have realized that you are the cause of everything that has gone wrong in my life. I am now ashamed to call you my mother. You have no control over my life, and you will never have. You did not make me who I am. I worked hard for every penny I got. I am ungrateful? You are selfish, wicked, and ungrateful," he shouted back at his mother.

Bob and Yusuf were standing close to the gate as they watched the heated drama unfold.

Rita was shocked at what was coming out of the mouth of her son. Her breathing increased. No one had ever talked to her that way before, and she'd never expected it from her own son. It struck at her bones. She was furious.

"How dare you insult me in that manner? Have you gone mad? How dare you accuse me of being wicked, selfish, and ungrateful? Your own mother! Are you out of your mind?"

She raised her right hand up and almost slapped her son, but Emeka held her hand in mid-air and stopped her.

"Enough, Mother! And how dare you barge into my house and accuse me of a crime I didn't commit?" He looked into her eyes. "Never raise your hands on me again. Whatever your plan, you have failed woefully. I will no longer allow you to destroy my life. Right now, you are no more needed in my house. You must go back to wherever you came from. I said enough is enough! Leave my life alone, and go and focus on your own marriage."

Rita was lost for words. Emeka's words shook in her mind like an earthquake. All at once, she began to tremble; she desperately clutched her hands on her chest, gasping for air.

Emeka noticed what was happening. "What is wrong, Mama?"

"My heart! I can't breathe!" she said in a panicked voice. Her eyes were filled with fear. She held her chest with a death grip and instantly tumbled and fell on the ground.

"Mama!" Emeka shouted, but his mother had already fainted.

"Bob! Yusuf!!"

He was frantic. Bob helped him to quickly carry his mother inside the car. They both entered the vehicle, Bob in the driver's seat.

"To the Rose Hill Hospital," Emeka shouted to him.

Immediately, the car sped out of the compound.

I can't lose my mother. He brought out his mobile phone. His hands began to twitch as he searched for Dr. Robert's phone number. His mind was filled with guilt. *Oh my God! What have I done?*

CHAPTER NINETEEN

Rose Hill Hospital, Port Harcourt

Rose Hill Hospital was busy with activity this Sunday evening. Emeka had been pacing around outside the room where his mother was being treated. He stared at the time—nine p.m. He had already told Bob to go and get him food and to inform his father about the incident. He was restless, his eyes filled with regret.

Inside the ward, Rita Obi was lying down on a white hospital bed, unconscious. She had been fitted with I.V. tubes connected to a monitor. Dr. Robert made an incision with a needle and inserted a small tube into her wind pipe through the front of her of her neck. Nurses in white and blue tunics attended to her as she continued to battle for her life.

Emeka watched as the door opened and the doctor's short and heavy frame stepped out. He measured Emeka for a long moment with big eyes behind thick glasses.

"Tell me what happened again," Dr. Robert said.

Emeka stopped pacing around and faced the doctor. *I need to calm down*, he reassured himself. "Doctor, it looks strange to me. We were arguing and shouting. It was heated. We have never had that kind of argument before. Suddenly, she tumbled down on the ground and fainted."

Dr. Robert maintained a calm expression on his face. "Any medical condition I should know of? Like asthma or hypertension?"

"I don't think so, Doctor." He thought over it for a while. The more he thought about it, the more he found out that he didn't know much about his mother like he thought he did. "I have always known my mother as a strong woman. She is hardly sick. Asthma? No. Hypertension? I am not sure. My father will know better. He will be here tomorrow."

The doctor removed his glasses and brought out a white handkerchief from his pocket which he used to clean his eyes. "She suffered from a mild heart attack. No test or diagnosis has been done yet to ascertain the cause. For the last three hours, we have been trying to stabilize her. Right now, she is breathing with oxygen delivered through transtracheal oxygen therapy. We have given her Nitro-glycerine."

"What does that do?" Emeka asked.

"It reduces the heart's work load and improves blood flow through the coronary arteries."

"Please, Doctor, do everything you can to save the life of my mother. I can't lose her. Thank you, Doctor," Emeka said in a desperate tone, his face dripping with sweat.

"Don't thank me yet. I will do my best," the doctor said as he went back into the room. He sighed and said in his mind, *Rich people and their troubles*.

***

The next day, Emeka was not able to go to his office. Throughout that Monday morning, he had been getting a lot of calls from his office, but he kept rejecting them. Because he didn't believe in mixing work with personal issues, he refused to tell anyone in the company about his mother.

He stayed by her side 'til Monday afternoon. It was a sunny day, the sunlight already streaking in through the windows. The nurses in the ward had reduced to just one.

Someone knocked on the door, and the young nurse went to open. Emeka stood up from where he was sitting beside his mother's bed and looked up as a young man in his early twenties wheeled an old man on a wheelchair inside the room.

Sir Matthew Obi looked frail and weak, the wrinkles on his face now distinct. He looked far older than his age. Now seventy, a lot had changed in his appearance. He appeared weak, but something about his eyes made his usual gentle nature almost vanish.

"Papa," Emeka said with relief in his voice.

Matthew Obi quickly raised his right hand and cautioned in a sharp voice, "Don't!"

Emeka stared at his father in bewilderment. *This is strange.* His father had always been soft and gentle, but today, he was different.

"What is wrong with you?" His father's voice cut him off from his deep thoughts. He looked at his father, trying to figure out what he meant. "You chased your wife away because you said she was unable to bear you a child. You couldn't wait. You were not patient, just five years into your marriage, and you have given up on your wife."

His father's voice was anything but gentle. It was stinging.

"Are you God?" Matthew asked his son in a cracking voice. He was making a great effort to speak in a loud voice. "Is she the one that will put the child there? And then, the woman that finally bore you a son, you chased her away after killing the child."

"But I didn't do—"

"Don't you dare talk while I'm talking!" Matthew was fuming. "Your mother told me everything before she paid you that visit. Now you want to kill my own wife, and for what? You have already started tearing this family apart with your dangerous mind-set. It is not all about you, and it will never be. You are not the son that I gave birth to. You are destructive, and I will not allow you to destroy this family. We don't need you or your money. You are no longer my son. Get the hell out of this hospital. Nonsense!"

It was like Judgment Day. The whole thing looked surreal to Emeka. He felt powerless. He stared at his father in utmost disbelief and then stumbled out of the ward with great confusion and sadness in his eyes. His phone started ringing instantly. He picked it up as he continued his walk out of the hospital.

"Emeka Obi," he said.

"Sir, it's Stella."

He was surprised. "Oh, Stella, what is the problem?"

"Sir, you are needed at the office right now. Something big is going down here," she said in an anxious voice.

"I will be there," he said before ending the call.

Something big! What could that be? What just happened at the hospital right now?

Emeka's mind was filled with lots of unanswered questions as he entered his car. "Bob, home first to shower and freshen up and then to the office."

He was very tired. Instantly, a thought entered his mind. Oh my God! *Is that what is happening?* He remembered. Oh, shit!

CHAPTER TWENTY

Emeka and Sons Headquarters, Port Harcourt
"Shall we begin?"

The voice of Mark Lang hovered across the vast conference room located inside the company's headquarters building.

"What is this meeting all about?" Emeka asked.

He was sitting on his executive chair, looking tired and annoyed. The twelve members of the board sat around the huge mahogany round table. Dr. Patricia Babatunde, the company's CFO, Paul Okoro, the company's marketing manager, Mark Lang, the company's COO, were all seated side by side. Other members included three top executives of the company and four top shareholders in the company.

These were people who jointly oversaw the activities of the company. All the members of the board wore serious faces, the atmosphere in the room highly tense. To his greatest surprise, Emeka discovered that Mark Lang had convened the meeting.

Mark stood up and faced the people in the round table. He opened a big file and began to speak.

"Ladies and gentlemen, I will not waste any of your time. Our company has been suffering huge losses for the past three years. The shareholders have been counting their woes in anger. Our customers have started to lose faith in us. We are having a bad year in the stock market. Our business opponents are smiling, and some have overtaken us. We have been losing a lot of contracts lately. Some of our businesses are no longer performing. These are our problems."

He paused for a moment and scanned the faces in the room. When he was sure they had digested his message, he continued.

"This company is suffering under the leadership of our current CEO. Lately, he has not been stable in his commitments. Poor management and passiveness have cost us lots of money. Our chairman is a good man and a good friend of mine, but personal interest and sentiments aside, this is business. This company doesn't belong to him anymore. It belongs to the shareholders.

"I called this emergency meeting for us to act. Some may advise we should lay off some workers, but I disagree. I support what most of you already want. We need a fresh hand at the top. Ladies and gentlemen, I propose a vote to remove Emeka Obi as the chairman of the board and the CEO of this company," Mark pronounced and sat down.

James Oladipo, a dark, bald man of average height and one of the top shareholders in the company and a member of the board, stood up immediately. He placed both hands on the thick round table. "Ladies and gentlemen, you have heard him. On the motion to remove Emeka Obi as our chairman and CEO, what say you? Aye or Nay?"

Emeka sat on his seat feeling powerless. The whole episode felt so unreal. He watched as the voting began.

"Aye" Mark said.

"Aye," Paul Okoro said.

"Nay," Dr. Patricia said.

"Aye."

"Nay."

"Aye."

"Aye."

Emeka's mind was far away. He was still thinking about the series of bad luck and problems he had been experiencing when he heard James's voice.

"Ladies and Gentlemen, the Nays have five votes while the Ayes have seven votes. The Aye carried the day. Mr. Emeka, the board has voted to remove you as chairman and CEO of this company."

It was like everything was happening in slow motion. The bigwigs on the board pulled in their weight and gave Mark their support. Mark was voted in as the new CEO and chairman of the board. Emeka sat down staring at the muraled wall as his world began to fall apart.

"As the chairman and CEO of this company," Mark was saying, "I have an urgent task of mending our image. With you cooperation, we will be back on our feet soon. We need to show a strong face to the world out there ..."

The rest of the meeting went fast like a blur.

When Emeka got back to his house, he took a cold bath, but he was still restless, a lot of thoughts colliding in his mind. *This is one of the disasters of letting the company go public. Now an outsider, a friend who betrayed my trust, is in charge of the company I built from scratch out of my own sweat. Did I make a mistake?*

He just didn't want to think about it anymore. As he was leaving his office earlier, he had gotten information from Stella that it was the big shareholders in the company with their huge wealth who wanted Mark to be in charge. Mark had somehow done a lot of lobbying.

The thought of Mark going behind his back to stage a corporate coup against him, to remove him from his position in the company, brought him a lot distress.

Emeka was angry because he was the one who'd brought Mark into his company. *He is far more ambitious than I thought.*

He closed his eyes and remembered the little exchange he'd had with Mark before he left the conference room. Mark had approached him. "Just to let you know, sir, it was nothing personal. This is for the progress of our company."

"No problem, Mark," he had said.

Mark had observed him for a moment with a concerned expression. "You look stressed out. Problems at home? Why don't you take some days off? It's the best therapy."

"I appreciate your concern, Mark," Emeka had told him.

Now, he felt so angry, helpless, annoyed, and lonely. He felt worn out. He began to think about his life and how everything had suddenly gone haywire. He felt he needed someone to talk to, someone that really cared.

All at once, he remembered his wife. He missed her so much. He recalled the good old days when they were so happy together. Then it dawned on him how he had lost his way and treated her badly, and he felt so guilty. Suddenly, his hands began to twitch violently.

Anita!

I am sorry, Anita. Life had been so difficult without you here. My wife! I need you now.

He opened his eyes instantly.

Oh my God! What have I done? I need to find my wife.

CHAPTER TWENTY-ONE

"Emeka, what have you gotten yourself into?"

It was Tuesday morning, the sky light blue, the streets of Port Harcourt already bustling with activity. Throughout the previous night, Emeka had not been able to sleep, the thoughts of Anita, his wife, troubling his mind. When he woke up, he felt so helpless. He needed a friend. He remembered Ben. They had not spoken for more than a year. Ben had been doing a supervisory work for his company at Abuja on a one-year programme.

Emeka had dialled his number, and he had picked up. Emeka was relieved when he discovered that Ben was back in the city. Immediately, he stepped into his car and drove down to Ben's residence at Rumuola. On meeting Ben in front of his house, he wasted no time in going straight to the matter troubling his mind.

"Ben, I need you to help me find my wife."

Ben was taken aback by his friend's request.

"Emeka, are you joking? Or are you crazy?" He observed his friend for a minute. A lot had changed in one year. "You look like you are fifty. Emeka, what is happening?"

And as they sat in Emeka's car, he poured out his mind to his friend. Ben listened intently for more than thirty minutes as the expression on his face changed from utter surprise, to shock, and to surprise again.

"Jesus! You stood helpless watching as your mother drove your wife out of your house! Look at how this sounds. Like crazy," Ben said in a raised voice.

"Ben, lower your voice. You are shouting. We are in the public," Emeka pleaded.

Ben smiled. He still looked young and handsome, his hair well shaved. He was dressed in white long sleeves and blue jean trousers. His big Timberland canvas and Rolex watch all made him appear larger than life; the big Port Harcourt boy. Emeka had not shaved for days; he was wearing a ruffled black shirt and brown trousers. He looked weary, stretched out, and older.

Benson looked at him and thought, *if this is what marriage entails, God, count me out.*

Right now, they were on their way to Elelenwo.

"Who did you say lives there again?" Benson asked.

"Her late aunt used to live there. Afterwards, Anita told me that her late aunt's younger sister was now residing there. That is definitely where she would be."

They passed lots of fruits sellers and pure water hawkers carrying their goods on the sidewalks. Emeka had been trying to find the right words to say to his wife. At first, he thought he would call her and apologize and tell her to come back home, but he had tried all her numbers—they were not available. He had asked her friends around the house if they had seen her; they said no while casting suspicious glances.

All of a sudden, the whole thing had turned into something bizarre. Now, he was searching for his wife. It felt so unreal to him. He drove for another two minutes before he finally reached Elelenwo.

When he reached the house, he parked the car, and they came out. They entered the compound, climbed the stairs, and in no time, he was knocking at the door.

The door opened, and they stared at the face of a fat black woman.

Strange. I have never seen this black woman before. He brought out Anita's picture and showed her. "I came to see this woman. She is a relative of her aunt, Bennet. I wonder if she is staying here."

The woman's face suddenly contorted, the sweat on her forehead mingled with the deep wrinkles on her face.

"You people again. What is this nonsense all about?" she shouted and looked back. "Papa Otunbo, this time it's a man. Can't they leave us alone?" She faced them again. "She is not staying here. Can't you people understand?"

Ben thought about something she said and raised his right hand for the woman to allow him to talk. "Wait a minute, you said 'you people again'. Which people? Has someone come here before?"

The woman shot them a surprise glance. "Yes, of course, this woman in the picture. She was here sometime last year. She was asking me the same thing. She was looking for Aunt Bennet's younger sister. They are no longer here. You should leave us alone."

Emeka became instantly curious. "Madam, she came here? You saw her? Where is she?"

The woman's expression changed to that of anger.

"You are asking me? She left. Don't disturb us again, or I will call police for you people." And she slammed the door at their faces.

Both friends looked at themselves, their eyes wide. They had gone back to Square One.

Benson was in deep thought. "If she came here, it means she was looking for somewhere to stay."

"Shit!! I'm sorry, Anita."

Emeka was babbling in deep regret.

"Quit bringing out chicken tears. Be a man and face the reality. You said she teaches at which school again?"

"Grace Royal College," he blurted out.

In the next two minutes, they were on their way to Grace Royal College at Borokiri.

Borokiri neighbourhood was situated south of old G.R.A, bounded by Ahoada Street to the north, Okrika Island to the east, Orubiri oilfield to the south, and Ship Builders Road to the west. A lot had changed in Borokiri over the years. The mere village which comprised of mostly farmlands decades ago had now turned into an industrial and commercial area.

Emeka drove past Enitonna High School and around Nigeria Navy School before stopping in-front of a huge metal gate. Grace Royal College was a private school owned by a big church in the city. Soon, they were asking some of the teachers questions.

"Anita, such a young lady, so calm and gentle. She is good with the students. I haven't seen her for some months now," a tall, dark man in his early forties said. His name was Samson, and he'd introduced himself as the Maths teacher.

"Anita, I know her, always kept to herself. One day, she suddenly disappeared," a chubby woman in the SS3 class, the biology teacher, said.

They met with a middle-aged woman in JSS1. She introduced herself as Madam Favour, wore thick glasses, and called herself a friend of Anita. "Anita, such a lovely woman! Do you know where she is?" she asked them back.

"Emeka, I'm tired. We are on a wild goose chase. I am not good at this kind of thing."

"Me, too, Ben," he said.

"Hi." It was a soft female voice. They both turned back at once. She was a fair young woman in her late twenties. "I heard you are looking for Anita."

"Yes," both men replied at once. "You know where she is?" Emeka asked.

"You can call me Ifeoma. I am not a teacher here, just the school typist." Both Emeka and Ben nodded. They listened intently. "We were good friends when she was here; we discovered that we share a lot of things in common. She was someone that I could really talk to. Before she stopped coming to school, she was always crying. She refused to open up to me, but as a woman, I knew that something was deeply wrong. It was written all over her face. Anita used to be a happy, down to earth woman. She is a good person."

It was a lot to take in. Emeka's mind filled with a floodgate of memories. What he heard opened up a lot of past recollections so that for a moment, he forgot where he was.

Benson observed the woman and asked, "You said she stopped coming to school. What happened? Why?"

Ifeoma's expression changed, like she was remembering something she had locked away deep down in her mind. A sad expression touched her face. "Honestly, I don't know. I feel it had to do with whatever was eating her up. One day, she just resigned and left. Just like that. Some teachers thought she had gone crazy, but I knew there must be a reason. I knew something was not right. That day, there was so much pain in her eyes."

Emeka wiped out the sweat forming on his forehead. "Please, do you know where she might be now? Do you still communicate with her?"

"I don't know where she is. Her numbers are no longer in service, and she is no longer on Facebook or WhatsApp or on any social network that I use. I have searched for her to know if I could help. I felt her pain. But it was like she just disappeared. It's like she no longer exists. I haven't seen her or heard from her. No communication, nothing."

"Thank you, Miss." Emeka thanked her, and they left.

He decided to follow Benson to his house and rest. When they reached his house, Benson filled a glass with Hero beer and gave it to him inside the living room.

"You need this," Benson said in a low voice.

Emeka collected the glass and gulped it down at once.

Benson sat down on his sofa and sighed heavily. "Emeka, this is serious. Maybe you need to go to the police and report about a missing person—"

"No, never!" Emeka cut him off.

Oh, God I pray that this is a dream. I can't believe my wife is nowhere to be found.

CHAPTER TWENTY-TWO

Rose Hill Hospital, Port Harcourt
Sir Matthew Obi watched his wife as she continued to breathe, and he smiled. That Wednesday morning, he had just finished eating his breakfast. He had been with his wife in Rose Hill Hospital since Monday. The doctor and his nurses had been able to stabilize her. Now, she no longer needed the help of oxygen to breathe and could do so freely. An I.V. tube attached to her right wrist and connected to a drip supplied liquid food to her body.

My lovely wife. God, I pray that she wakes up.

She had yet to open her eyes. The doctor had told him that she would be conscious very soon. He sighed. His servant, Samuel, was sleeping on a long chair inside the ward. Soon, a nurse came and began to attend to the patient. She brought out a notepad and wrote down her observations.

"She is breathing fine. So far so good. Please let no one touch her," she said.

Mat nodded, and she left. He stayed by her bedside for the next two hours. He had a lot on his mind. Suddenly, the bed began to shake. He looked at his wife. Her body was quivering. Instantly, the alarm of the monitor started beeping.

Trouble!

"Doctor! Nurse!" he shouted, and in less than a minute, Dr. Robert and two of his nurses rushed inside the ward.

For the next ten minutes, they did their best to stabilize her. Mat watched as the doctor applied pressure on her chest for the third time with a defibrillator, and the patient coughed and opened her eyes.

"Thank God she is awake," Mat said, his face beamed.

The doctor and the nurses kept attending to her.

"You are fine, madam. Don't remove any of these," the doctor said.

Dr. Robert washed his hands in a small bowl inside the ward and cleaned them with a towel. He brought out a white handkerchief, removed his eye glasses, and cleaned his eyes. Then he put the glasses back on.

"Doctor, can I speak with her now?" Mat asked.

The doctor faced him. "Yes, sir, she is conscious now. I will give you a moment with her. After that, we will administer her some injections and allow her to rest."

"Thank you, Doctor."

The doctor smiled briefly and left the room. Mat held his wife's left hand, and she turned her head and faced him.

"Mat, is that you?" Her voice was weak.

"Yes, my dear, it's me."

"You are here, you came." A kind of delight tinged her voice now.

"Yes, I came. You know I will always be by your side. There is no place else I will rather be."

She forced herself to smile. Suddenly, tears began to streak down her cheeks.

Mat observed her and became concerned. "Mama Emeka, what is wrong?"

She tightened the grip on his hand. "Mat, I was so afraid. I thought I would die."

He heard panic in her voice.

"Me, too, dear. I was afraid you would die."

"I don't want to die yet. Not yet." She began to sob.

"My dear, you will not die. I am here with you."

"Really?" she asked.

Mat furrowed his brow." I don't understand."

"Promise me you will not leave my side no matter what happens," she said.

"My dear, I promise."

She lay still for a minute and said, "Mat, there is something I want to tell you."

He felt the pain in her voice. *And what would that be?*

"Samuel!" he called out. The young boy instantly woke up and looked at his master with mouth agape. "Leave us, stay outside."

Samuel got up and walked out of the room.

Mat faced his wife. "What is it, my dear?"

It took her a moment to speak.

"It's about the fertility test. Mat, I'm so sorry, you have to forgive me." She was sobbing.

"I don't understand." He had a confused expression on his face as his mind began to sort out his past memories.

"You don't remember? It was more than thirty-five years ago. Remember, when we were trying to get pregnant. For four years, we didn't conceive. We were worried. So we did a fertility test," she said, her voice more of a whisper.

Mat smelt something was wrong. "Yes, I remember."

She remained silent.

"What happened?"

"I paid the doctor to swap the results," she blurted out.

Mat felt like she had just dropped an atomic bomb.

"You did what?" he asked, the tension in his voice increasing.

"After we did the test, remember you told me to go and get the results in the hospital. You were going for a state meeting of secondary school principals. So I went and met the doctor in his office. He gave me the results, and out of curiosity, I opened the envelope and checked the results right there."

"And what happened?"

"I was fertile, but you were not. It pained me so much. And I didn't want you to be disappointed. I didn't want you to know that the cause of our infertility came from your side." Her voice cracked.

Mat sat motionless, his eyes darting left and right. "And what did you do, Rita?"

"I paid the doctor. I paid him to swap the results. I don't know how he did it, but he brought another one that said you were fertile. I took that one home. That was the one you saw."

"But you told me—"

"I lied."

Mat was suddenly afraid. He had always felt it, had always known that something was wrong with everything. All it took was for just one part of the wall to crack, and everything started crumbling down.

That's when he realized that her confession had a dangerous implication. Oh my God! His hands began to tremble when he realized what it meant.

"Rita, what have you done? Emeka! All those years, I thought I had a son, a child to call my own. My only son! And you were silent until now. Who is his father?"

Rita panicked. She felt she had no other choice. *I kept this from him for more than thirty-five years. I have been carrying a heavy weight in my heart. I have to release myself now from this burden. If I will die, let me die knowing that my conscience has stopped punishing me. I just want the nightmares to stop.*

"Patrick," she said.

Mat's body jerked up. "What?"

"You heard me."

"Which Patrick? There are a lot of Patricks."

"Your friend Patrick. I'm so sorry, Mat. It happened after we had gone for the test. There was a time you were not always around. You were always away. From this conference to that meeting, I was so lonely, and Pat was always coming to check if you were in the house. Sometimes afterwards, he would pity me and keep me company.

"I didn't want us to be childless. Knowing you were not fertile didn't help matters. One thing led to another, and we had a brief affair, and I got pregnant and had to make you believe it was yours. I didn't know how to tell you. I was afraid you would leave me. I couldn't go back to Patrick. He was married at that time. I am so sorry, Mat. You have to forgive me." She was weeping.

Mat's eyes widened. The expression on his face changed from utter surprise to shock to anger and then to hatred. His breathing had increased. His hands were trembling feverishly. The colours of his eyes had darkened.

When he stared into the eyes of his wife, Rita became so afraid. She had never seen her husband like that before. The look on his face was something else.

Mat felt betrayed by the two people closest to him. *My wife and my best friend! All these years wasted. All my efforts in vain! Everything I have suffered to build, all the sacrifices I have made. Oh my God! Patrick!*

He felt like he was losing his grip on everything. It was too much for him to bear. He tried to hold onto his wheelchair, but his hands were twitching too much. The wrinkles on his face contorted—so much hate and anger there.

He pointed his finger at his wife as he stared into her face with his bloodshot eyes. "You whore, you will die here alone. I will go now and begin to get ready for your funeral. Shameless woman!"

Rita was so afraid of her life after hearing what her husband told her. Her body began to tremble, and the alarm of the monitor started to beep.

"Samuel!" Mat shouted.

Samuel entered the room.

"Get me out of this place."

The alarm was now beeping incessantly. The doctor and two of his nurses rushed into the ward as Samuel wheeled his master out of the room and the hospital.

***

At the same time, Emeka was sitting on the huge bed inside his room typing fast on his laptop. He was still wrapped in his towel. He had just finished showering when he got the message that the package was ready for him.

It's show time.

He smiled as he clicked on 'accepted.'

It was now Wednesday afternoon, and the weather was bright and sunny. *I have to go now.* Throughout last night, he had been feeling so lonely and frustrated. He no longer went to his office. With nothing to do, his mind had wandered to other things.

I need to let out this steam and tension so bottled up inside me, he had told himself. *It's been too long since*

I've been with a woman. Not being able to find his wife had made him accept the fact that he had indeed lost her forever. *Oh! If she was here ...*

It was when he was checking his email that he saw the Ad; a classic hotel in Rumuola that could make his wishes come true. He had gone to the website, and the more he clicked through the pages, the more he became interested. He wasted no time in choosing his specifications: tall, dark, and curvy.

Perfect for my taste.

When he got the message from the website that they had gotten someone for him, he was so excited. *Someone with all my specifications*. He quickly accepted and paid for their services online with his debit card. He shut down his laptop and quickly put on a red polo and black jean trousers.

In the next three minutes, he was on his way to Eleganza Hotel at Rumuola. He cursed out loud as the huge traffic in Rumuola Road delayed him terribly. It took him one hour to reach his destination. He parked his car at the garage.

Eleganza Hotel was a two-storey building decorated with flowers. They boasted of fulfilling the dark desires of their exclusive customers. You could only book for their services online. 'Your privacy is our watchword,' said their conspicuous motto.

Emeka got out of the car, approached the brick building, and pushed in through the heavy door. He gave the receptionist his identification tag number which he'd gotten after he'd accepted the tempting offer at their website. The receptionist gave him a key.

"Go up. Room 101. Your partner will join you shortly." That was all she said. No greeting—all professional. Exactly how Emeka liked it.

He climbed up to the tiled floor and searched for his room. He found it at the extreme, unlocked the door, and entered into the tastefully furnished room decorated with a Persian rug and expensive furniture. The walls had wallpapers all showing a view of the Pacific Ocean. A blue light illuminated the room. The windows were closed with their shutters drawn.

Emeka smiled and quickly began to undress. He unbuttoned his shirt, removed his trousers and shoes, and climbed on the big bed. *Now, I will wait.*

Kpom! Kpom!

A gentle knock came from the door. He smiled knowingly—he hadn't locked the door. "Please come in."

The door opened, and a tall, curvy lady entered the room, dressed in a sexy, seductive attire. Her transparent silky top only helped to reveal that she wore just a strapless bra and G-string, her backside bare and inviting. All the efforts had been put in place for the pleasure of her customer. She approached him like a shark waiting to devour her prey. Emeka observed her closely, grinning widely as his partner stepped into the blue light.

Suddenly, their eyes met, and a quick flash of recognition passed. Emeka's body instantly became rigid, his face drained of blood.

"Oh my God!" they both gasped.

CHAPTER TWENTY-THREE

Eleganza Hotel, Port Harcourt

"Anita!" Emeka exclaimed. "Jesus! I have been looking for you. What are you doing in this kind of place?"

It was his wife—he could see her clearly now. She had become a prostitute with heavy makeup on her face.

She glanced at him with angry eyes. "And what are you doing here? Are you not supposed to be with your mother and your whore?"

Emeka quickly climbed off the bed, and they both stared at each other.

"It's complicated," he said as he glanced down.

When he looked at her face again, he began to notice a change. Her carefully constructed exterior suddenly started to crack, and she burst into tears.

"See what you have done to me. You chose your mother over me and abandoned me when you knew I had nothing. I had no one. You put me in this condition. I suffered just to stay alive."

Emeka felt so terrible, he was lost for words. He thought about his condition and looked at his wife and how she'd had to stoop so low just to survive, and tears began to drop from his eyes.

I ... am ... so ... sorry, Anita," he sobbed. "Yes, I am responsible for your present condition. I am sorry. I am sorry for all the things I have done. I made a terrible mistake, and I will live with it for the rest of my life."

They both sat down on the bed as he began to tell her all that he had gone through.

"Right now, my mother is unconscious in the hospital, my father has disowned me, the baby is dead, and I don't know where the girl is. And the worst of all is that I have been removed as the CEO and Chairman of the board of my company. My friends have deserted me. Even my own family is against me. My life is completely in chaos," he said in tears.

Anita wiped her tears and continued to stare at her husband. She discovered that he had changed. He looked weary, and she felt pity for him. When she remembered all that she had gone through because of what he had done to her, she felt like crying again. As she looked into his eyes, she realized that she still loved him.

"I am sorry, Anita. I have been a terrible husband. I am ready to be the husband that I haven't been for a long time, a husband that deserves your love. Life has been hell without you. All the sharks have closed in on me. I need you back in my life, Anita. I love you so much. I miss you so much that it hurts," he pleaded, and they leaned closer and hugged each other tightly, both of them sobbing.

"Oh, Emeka, I miss you, too. You can't imagine what I've gone through." She started sobbing as she held him tightly.

At that moment, the mobile phone in one of the pockets of Emeka's trousers began to ring. He ignored it, but it continued to ring, shattering their sudden reunion. He brought out his phone and picked the call. "Hello."

"Please, is this Mr Emeka?" a female voice asked anxiously at the other end of the line.

On alert, he replied, "Yes, who is this?"

"Please, I am a nurse in St. Louis Hospital at Diobu. Someone was involved in an accident here. It's been quite long. Since yesterday, we have been calling the numbers on the phone with the hope of connecting with someone close to the patient. This morning, an old couple arrived at the hospital, perhaps the parents. They insisted we should call you."

Emeka's body stiffened. Anita looked at him and was concerned.

"Please, what exactly happened? Who is the person? I ... don't ... understand ..."

"Please, you are needed at St. Louis Hospital in Diobu right now," the female voice said, and the call ended.

Emeka's body jerked in pain as he rushed like a man-on-the-run, struggling to put on his clothes.

Anita was worried. "Emeka, what is the problem?"

"Honey! Something came up. I don't understand it yet. I have to attend to something right now. It's urgent," he babbled as he put on his clothes. He suddenly collected his thoughts and said, "Please leave this place."

He quickly took her number.

"Wait for my call," he added.

She suddenly stood up. "No, there is something I want to tell you. You have to know, Emeka."

Her face grew tense, her voice insistent.

"It will have to wait," he said as he rushed out of the room.

He climbed down the stairs quickly and unlocked his car, then started it and drove off. What happened?

An idea entered his mind, and he shuddered at the thought.

***

Rose Hill Hospital, Port Harcourt

Dr. Robert was in his office glancing at the time. Two p.m. The Wednesday sun had been very hot; even the air conditioner he'd had installed had malfunctioned. Was it the heat that spoiled it? His thoughts took him to the event of the previous day.

What a family!

He'd remembered that as they rushed into the ward. He had been surprised to see her husband leaving the hospital. The old man was angry, he had observed. When they reached the patient, she had been trembling. He'd noticed the unusual expression on her face. *Was she frightened? Scared of what?*

It took them an hour to stabilize her. *What is really happening?* He had conducted a lot of tests to know what really triggered the heart attack. He had to do another diagnosis because something was wrong. Initially, he had ruled it as an ordinary heart attack and had been giving her medications to stamp out the symptoms and get her back on her feet.

Later, he'd discovered to his greatest dismay that the medications were only a temporary relief. They were able to stabilize her, but soon after, he'd noticed that something was terribly wrong. Shortly afterwards, she stopped responding to treatment. He had seen the result of the other tests. He was now waiting for his head nurse to bring him the result of the blood test.

Soon, he would have a clearer view of what he was dealing with, he supposed. He became engrossed in his work.

The knock on his door came after an hour.

"Come in, Marty."

Marty, a slim nurse in her early forties, opened the door and gave him a manila file. "The blood test, sir."

"Thank you, Marty."

She nodded and left. Most of the documents were about the patient's glucose level, blood pressure, and general observations about her health. He brought out the main document—the result of the blood test, and began to read it.

Instantly, his face turned pale.

Oh, no! This can't be!

CHAPTER TWENTY-FOUR

Diobu, Port Harcourt

Diobu was a densely populated neighbourhood located within the heart of the city—the home of most rising music stars and famous soccer talents like Joseph Yobo and Duncan Mighty. Its borders comprised of New G.R.A to the north, D-line to the northeast, Old G.R.A to the east, and Eagle Island to the South West.

Most of the commercial activities existing in Diobu had been brought about by its numerous markets. Diobu was also home to the infamous 'Mile One,' one of the largest open-air markets in the city. Although the neighbourhood was one of the most commercially vibrant areas in the city, it was actually the main jungle of Port Harcourt. With high rates of gang activities, kidnapping, and armed robberies, Diobu remained one of the most dangerous neighbourhoods in the city.

Who could this individual be, and what was the person doing in a place like this? Emeka continued to wonder. *What has this person got to do with me?* It had taken him one and half hours to navigate through the heavy traffic in the city. He passed St. Paul's Anglican School and stopped in front of St Louis Hospital. He opened the front door and met with the nurse at the Reception desk, a young lady in white tunic.

"Hi, please, I was called to come to this hospital. I ... don't know—" Emeka stopped talking.

Her face brightened. "You are Mr. Emeka?"

"Yes."

"I was the one who called you. Please, follow me."

They cut through a lot of corridors and entered inside a room close to a bend. All the patients in the room had white sheets covering their faces. Emeka heard some stifled cries and shuddered.

"Let me take you to the couple. They insisted I should call you."

They moved towards an elderly couple sobbing close to a bed. A doctor in white coat was trying to comfort the woman.

The young nurse approached them. "Emeka is here."

They nodded, and she left.

The couple looked far older than he thought. The fight had gone out in them. A young lady was also with them. They looked familiar. A family? Emeka was searching the memories in his mind.

The old woman stared at Emeka with a painful expression on her face and pointed at him. "You! You did this to our daughter."

"Calm down. Everybody is looking at us," her husband said.

"I don't understand. What is going on here?" Emeka asked.

The old man rested his gaze on him. "It's Amaka."

Emeka felt a sudden rush of blood up his spine. "What happened?"

"We are her parents. This is her elder sister, Amara," the man said, pointing at a young girl beside him.

Emeka nodded.

The doctor, a dark man of average height, said, "She had an accident."

"Oh, God, no!" Emeka cried out.

"The witnesses said she has been wandering around the streets of Diobu since Monday. As she was crossing the road, a truck hit her. I'm so sorry. She died instantly."

Emeka felt his legs go weak.

"This is her. We will soon take her to the morgue," the doctor continued as he showed Emeka to the bed.

He approached the bed. A white sheet covered her body. He uncovered her face and almost fainted. Her innocent features were covered in blood, some parts of her head broken. Her mouth lay agape, with terror in her eyes.

He put his hands on his head and turned his face away.

The old woman was pointing her finger at him accusingly. "You have taken our daughter away from us. You led her to her death."

The old man held his wife on his shoulder. "She was always telling us of how bad you treated her. We told her to come back home to Enugu, but she refused. She didn't want to disappoint your mother."

The old man looked down as he brought out a handkerchief and wiped his eyes.

Emeka stood rooted to the ground.

"When you didn't want my sister anymore, you could have brought her back to us at Emene. You just threw her away like a piece of rag. You didn't mind that she didn't know anyone in the city. Now, she is dead," their daughter tearfully added.

Emeka felt so awful. "I am so sorry. I know your family will never forgive me. I'm so sorry. It was never my intention to stay with her. My mother imposed her on me ..." Emeka found himself stammering. He thought about what he said and regretted it. "Never mind, I am so overwhelmed by what happened. Oh, God!"

He knelt down and broke down in tears. *How much pain can a man take?* he asked himself. *This is way too much.*

Suddenly, there was a commotion. An argument. "No, we shouldn't. He doesn't deserve it."

"Yes, he should. He needs to know." The old couple were talking in stifled voices.

"I have made up my mind," the man said. "Young man, come here," he called Emeka.

Emeka stood up and approached them, his eyes wide.

"I am supposed to hate you for what you did to my daughter," the old man was saying. "You were wicked to her, but that is between you and your God. I won't judge you. I am now an old man. I have seen a lot of things. Life had been so unfair to us. Such a senseless death!"

He paused for a moment and continued. "There is nothing new under the sun. However, you are not the only one to share the blame for what happened to our daughter. We share part of the blame, too. We gave her to your parents. We were supposed to meet you first. But we rushed things, and we paid the price. You didn't pay the bride price; your parents did it on your behalf. Everything was so wrong from the beginning."

The old man stopped, his eyes fixed in a black stare at the opposite wall. "We wanted her to get married so desperately that we forgot to do things in order. We didn't even know if you were interested in our daughter. It was only the bride price that was paid. There was no wedding. That should have brought us back to our senses, but we were numb. And when you were treating her badly, we were supposed to ignore your mother's assurances and come and take her home, but we didn't. We failed her."

The old man began to sob silently as he held his wife. He wiped his tears and said, 'Let's leave this place. Nothing can bring her back. Follow us. There is something we want to show you."

He followed the three of them as they stepped outside the room. They passed through the corridor at the right and climbed up the stairs, then entered the first room by the left, which was tastefully furnished. *A visitor's room?* Emeka followed them and entered.

"Show him," the old man said to his daughter.

The young girl nodded and showed Emeka a small baby basket on top of the bed. Emeka was instantly startled. The baby basket looked familiar. Amara, the young lady, bent down and brought out a baby who began to cry.

Emeka stood motionless. *This can't be.*

The young lady was smiling. "What a miracle, right? God saved him. The witness said Amaka left him in the basket at a corner of the road and rushed to cross when the accident happened. Amaka's body and the baby were then brought to the hospital, the nearest hospital they could find."

"Yes," the father said. 'It's Amaka's baby, your son."

Emeka looked at the man with a confused expression. "I don't understand. I thought the baby was dead."

The old woman came closer and collected the baby from her daughter. "No. The baby is alive. Such a lovely child! Less than a week old. My late daughter was tired of the way you were treating her. She was always calling to tell us you had rejected her. You were treating her badly. So she faked the baby's death to escape from you. She knew that if she made you believe that the baby was dead, you may chase her away because she won't tie you down with the baby again, and you proved her right."

Emeka opened his mouth to say something but closed it.

The old man said to him, "The baby is yours. It will also remind all of us of Amaka. Take care of the baby and redeem yourself from your past mistakes."

Emeka collected the baby from the woman and held it in his arms. He was surprised that the baby didn't cry. He looked at his face, so tender. It had a flawless complexion, not too dark, and he could see the stark resemblance. The baby stared back at him with his small eyes and began to giggle softly, unaware of all the tragedies, drama, and pain that surrounded him.

Emeka felt like the hands of the clock should go back so that he could start afresh to a time when none of these had happened.

"I will take care of the baby. I promise with every fibre in my body. I will spend the rest of my years making amends to this child. The errors of the past will not be repeated again. I will do things right this time," he said firmly.

"I hope so, son," the old man said.

"We are all family now," Emeka said as he greeted them all.

It was already four p.m., and Emeka agreed to take them to his house. They would stay 'til tomorrow. When they were ready, they could go back home to Emene in Enugu.

As he drove them back to his house, he did everything to fight back tears that kept trying to force themselves out of his eyes.

Twisted

CHAPTER TWENTY-FIVE

Trans-Ekulu, Enugu

It was Wednesday evening, and the sun was about to set. Sir Matthew Obi was eating mango fruit inside his compound at Enugu. It had been raining since morning. Up 'til now, a heavy wind still blew. The dark clouds had not yet cleared, making the weather a bit cold.

Immediately after he had stormed out of the hospital on Tuesday morning, Samuel had driven him back to Enugu in his Mercedes-Benz, a car that Emeka had bought for him on his sixty-ninth birthday. Samuel also acted as his driver.

Mat was no longer angry at his son. *He was not really my son. Rita! That woman has destroyed everything.* He finished the mango he was eating and waited. He had already told Samuel to invite his friend Patrick to his house. They normally saw each other on Sunday and Wednesday evenings—old men chit chat.

He will be here soon, Mat thought as he fumed with anger. At this point, he wanted to stop fighting and give up and let them win, but he wanted to see the look on his friend's face. At first, he didn't believe it, but then, life was a bitch.

He remembered his late father's last words. 'Trust no one but yourself.' His father had been the kind of man who saw only the good in people. He was fun to be with and thought everyone was like him. He was a trader in Onitsha in the sixties, but later went bankrupt after he was betrayed by his friends. He died a miserable death.

Maybe it was fate, Mat thought.

Instantly, a knock on the gate interrupted him from his deep thoughts. He looked on as Samuel opened the gate and Patrick entered. Patrick's potbelly showed clearly on his blue Niger-Delta attire. He wore a long blue shirt on blue trousers.

"Mat, I was worried. You came back quickly. Is there something wrong? How is she doing?" he asked as he approached his friend.

Suddenly, the expression on Mat's face changed. All his feelings of pain and hatred had returned. He remembered what his friend had done and fumed in rage. Patrick panicked when he saw the vicious glare in his friend's eyes.

Before Pat could answer the questions on his mind, Mat had wheeled up his wheelchair in his direction; he was holding a stick and rushing to hit him. The wheelchair careened down in full force now. Patrick acted on impulse and dodged the incoming onslaught at the last minute. The wheelchair continued to move fast until Mat lost control of it and it hit a tree directly at his front.

"Papa!" Samuel saw it too late. When he reached his master, the wheelchair had hit the tree hard, toppling him down in the process. Mat was on the ground cursing out loud and in a lot of pain.

Oh! If it was when I was much younger. He groaned. Patrick approached him as Samuel lifted the wheelchair and helped his master to sit on it.

Patrick gave his friend an inquisitive, searching look.

"You know," he said. His face was filled with painful regret.

Mat glared at Patrick. "You are heartless, a green snake in green grass. I took you as a brother. In fact, you are a part of my family, and you betrayed my trust."

"I am sorry, Mat."

"For over thirty-five years, you kept this from me."

"I knew this day would come. It pains me more than anything. I still regret it up 'til today." Mat remained silent. Patrick continued. "It was never my intention to have an affair with your wife. She was the one that planned it all. It was her. And it cost me my marriage. I have paid the price, and I am still paying the price. I could never forgive myself for what I did to you. I didn't tell you because I was afraid it will destroy your marriage. I am so sorry."

"Samuel!" Mat called out.

Samuel rushed to his master's side. Mat had heard enough. He was tired of it all. "Take this man out of my compound," he commanded.

Samuel led the panic-stricken Patrick out of the compound and closed the gate. He then helped Mat into the house. He took him to his room and helped him lie on the bed.

Mat felt so weak, his leg hurting him. He quickly reached for some pain relievers he normally kept by his bedside and put two in his mouth. He collected bottled water at the side of his bed and gulped it down.

Rita! He stared blankly at the wall. *I shouldn't have given in to my parents. I shouldn't have cancelled the wedding.*

***

Choba, Port Harcourt

Choba Junction in Port Harcourt was a very busy area, particularly this Wednesday evening. As Bob looked for where to park the car, hawkers of all sorts of goods came rushing to their side.

"Keeping moving, Bob," Emeka said.

With all that he had gone through lately, he was supposed to be reasonably tired, but not on this evening. He had already called Anita. She was waiting for him at the junction. He was so excited and looked forward to seeing her.

"Where should I park?" Bob asked.

"We are not parking. There is no place to park here. Keep going. She will be somewhere here at Choba. We will see her soon."

All of a sudden, Emeka heard someone calling his name. He looked at the direction and saw Anita. She wore a pink top on tight blue jean trousers. He felt his body jerk up in excitement.

"It's okay, stop the car. Anita is here."

Bob stopped the car and helped Anita put her bags in the trunk. Immediately after she entered the car, Emeka leaned forward and crushed his mouth on hers in an urgent kiss, hard and forceful.

Anita closed her eyes as she enjoyed the moment. Suddenly, she felt Emeka removing her hands from her body.

"See that truck. Go, go, go!" he ordered. Bob started the car and was able to dodge the oncoming truck in time.

"Darling, I am so happy that you are here," Emeka said as he held his wife. He was happy when he felt the ring on her finger. He also had a list of unanswered questions, but he skipped them. He didn't want to spoil the moment.

Anita held him tightly. Suddenly, she removed his hands from her body. Emeka was surprised. The expression on her face changed. She raised her right hand and slapped her husband.

Emeka flinched. "For what?"

"Don't leave me again," she said and then hugged him tightly.

They reached home by four-thirty p.m. Bob and Yusuf were so happy that their madam was back. They greeted her with smiles on their faces and carried her bags inside.

When the couple reached the room, Emeka faced his wife.

Anita knew what was coming. "First, before you say anything, there are some things I want to tell you."

"Go ahead," he said.

"I have been staying with Chimdi, a friend of mine in Rumuomasi. I did a lot of odd jobs before I started this one. They have been telling me about it for the past six months, convincing me to join them. It took me time to make up my mind. I was somehow waiting for you. Sometimes, I would dream of you coming to take me back. But you didn't come back. Then, I finally lost hope and changed my contacts. I just started last week. You were my first customer."

Emeka kept quiet for a moment. "Is that all?"

"There is something else. I don't know how you will take it."

He flinched. His instincts told him it would be something big. Perhaps she'd slept with a lot of guys.

"What is it?" he asked, his voice louder.

"It's about Benson," she replied quietly.

Emeka became highly alert. "You mean my friend Benson?"

"Yes."

"What about Benson?"

"The call-girl stuff at Eleganza Hotel, Benson is the one that runs it. He controls the girls and pays them. He was the one that set it up for me. I later found out that my friend Chimdi was a call-girl working for Benson at the hotel."

Emeka sat down on the bed at once. What he'd just heard made him catch his breath. He remembered something. "No, it's not true, Anita. Benson was away for the past year. He just came back from Abuja. I don't believe it. Are you sure it's Benson?"

"You can check my phone and see his number. I can show you the messages he sent to me telling me to make up my mind on time. Benson and some of his friends own the hotel. He also arranges girls for the big men in Port Harcourt. He hangs out with the big guys. In fact, Benson has been in the city for the past six months. He was always coming to give us money to buy food. He took care of us."

Emeka was confused. *Benson! Jesus Christ! That's probably how he was able to keep up with his expensive lifestyle.* His eyes filled with rage. "Honey, just undress and relax. I'm coming."

I know where to find him.

"Emeka, don't do something stupid," Anita shouted.

Three minutes later, Emeka was already on his way to Benson's house at Rumuola. He got there by six p.m. and kept banging on the gate.

"Who is that? Who is that?" Benson was shouting.

He opened the gate, and Emeka barged in forcefully. Benson was bare-chested, wearing only knickers. From the way he sounded, Emeka felt he was semi-drunk. *Maybe he had been drinking.*

Emeka charged towards him and punched him hard in the stomach. "My so-called friend! So you knew all along. You have been in this city all along, and you have been with my wife for the past six months. You stupid son of a bitch, and you even followed me to search for her."

Emeka dashed towards him again, but Benson dodged him this time.

Benson coughed. "I heard about what happened. You came to Eleganza and met your wife. All of this are not my fault, Em! We cater for men like you, those that are frustrated in their marriage, that no longer enjoy the love at home. Those that marriage has badly destroyed, those that their wives don't have time for them, that are tired of eating the same food for twenty years. They want something different, not the same old conventional routine. It gets boring. I started this when I looked around and saw what marriage was doing to my fellow men. Look at you, Emeka."

Benson gave a crooked laugh. "I know how you looked so fresh and cute before your marriage. Look at what marriage has done to you. I am so sorry, Emeka, it was just bad luck, a stroke of fate, that both of you had to find each other at Eleganza."

Emeka looked on in dismay as he witnessed his friend changing entirely in front of him. "That's why you never wanted to marry. Because you were afraid of what marriage would do to you. So you knew where she was all this time."

He rushed at Ben and this time grappled him on his neck. He tightened the grip.

"I am sorry. Look, she just started. You are her first customer," Ben managed to say.

Suddenly, he stamped his right leg hard on Emeka's left leg, and Emeka winced in pain as he released his hold.

Ben laughed. "Look at you, Emeka. You are now so weak. You just spoiled my business. I was supposed to use her to make a lot of money."

Emeka's blood boiled. He charged up at Ben and toppled him to the ground. Ben cried out as Emeka continued to punch him hard everywhere, blow after blow.

"You spineless fool. Have you been sleeping with my wife? You knew she was down." Emeka gripped him on the neck again and squeezed hard. "Have you been taking advantage of her?"

Ben punched him hard on the stomach, and Emeka fell on the ground, covering his mid-section with his hands in great pain. Ben stood up, staggering left and right, blood coming out of his mouth.

"I am tired of carrying all the blame. You were the one that chased your wife away. Emeka, you abandoned her. I was the one that gave her shelter and food and provided her with a means of survival. How was she supposed to survive with the ten thousand Naira they were paying her in the school? In this city, that money is fucking change! She was going to earn a lot of money had she worked for me. You should be thanking me."

Emeka lunged at him and landed a heavy blow on his face. "You son of a bitch!"

"What the hell!" Benson put his finger in his bloody mouth. "Oh my God! Emeka, you just broke my teeth. You have turned into a monster. You chased your wife away, got another woman pregnant, killed her baby, and chased *her* away. You even tried to kill your mother. And now, you want to kill me!"

Emeka slammed a vicious blow on his stomach. "The baby is still alive, fool. I didn't kill anyone. Who knows? Maybe you will be dead by the time I finish with you."

Benson's eyes filled with fear. He stood up and ran towards the gate and stopped, facing Emeka.

"It's not my fault. I came to visit one of my call-girls, and your wife, Anita, was with her. I was even surprised to see her there. She cried out and told me all the bad things you did to her. I almost cried, too. I took pity on her. I understood her pain. All the time she was with you, she was staying in a negative environment. You turned a young, happy, and cheerful woman into a sad soul tormented by bad memories you visited upon her.

"Chimdi and I decided to give her something meaningful. Things are difficult, and it's not everybody that can survive in this city. Some people die of starvation because they don't have enough money. It took us a lot of time to convince her to work for us, and she later agreed. But you came and spoiled everything. Just like the way you came into her life and later abandoned her. Everywhere you go, you leave a trail of destruction."

Emeka stood up and rested his back against the wall. He was in a lot of pain. He felt heartbroken as he stared at Ben who was now far away from his reach. "You wild scum, I trusted you, and you did this to me. You told me you travelled. I believed all the lies. All this time, you had found my wife and you were preparing her, getting her ready to be your whore. You shameless fool."

"What will you have me do, mama's boy? You were with another woman. Your mum was suddenly the lord of your house. I actually came one day and saw the two women, and I had to go. You chose your mother over your wife, and yet, you blame me. That was your mistake, not mine. You didn't even make an effort to look for her then. It was after a year that you woke up from your slumber; when you had driven your mistress away and had put your mother in the hospital. Good husband! Back then, what would you have me do? Bring her back? You no longer wanted her. I had no choice but to be a good friend and take care of her."

Emeka was dumbfounded for a while, then he collected his thoughts.

"You think you are smart. You changed her phone and Sim-card so that no one would reach her, and you call yourself a friend!" Emeka fired back at him.

"Yes, we gave her a new identity. We changed everything, and she became completely a new person. She even gave herself a new name when I told her that you had gotten your mistress pregnant and would no longer come for her. Oh, I knew. She cried when she realized you had forgotten her. It gave her a new confidence to agree to work with us.

"We made her a new person. We had to do it for her because her old identity was killing her inside. You mended her heart when you met her and tore it apart when you abandoned her. She told me everything. She was always having sleepless nights, crying and sobbing. You were holding her back. It was like she was stuck in the past. A past you used to torment her. You don't understand, do you? You were the reason for her pain. We had to bring her back to the present and back to life."

Emeka felt weak. *No more*, he said in his mind. *I don't want to fight anyone again. I will not die before my time.*

He checked his shirt. The buttons had been torn off by Benson. He staggered to the gate and looked at his friend one last time. "Stay away from me and my family. I don't want you near my wife again, else this city won't accommodate the both of us."

Benson watched him in fear as he stepped out of the gate and drove his car into the busy road.

Ben hit his head with his right hand; he had a lot of shame and regret in his eyes. *What a mess!* he thought as he walked slowly into his house.

CHAPTER TWENTY-SIX

"Good morning, beautiful," Emeka said to Anita as he kissed her on the forehead.

She opened her eyes and smiled. The Thursday morning sun rays had already started streaking in through the window, trying to blind their vision.

"What time is it?" she asked.

"It's already eight a.m."

"Hmm, we woke up late," she said.

"It's alright."

Anita sat on the bed. For the first time in a long time, they'd slept together peacefully—no quarrels, no arguments. She had been worried the previous night when her husband had come back home with his clothes dirty and torn. She knew what had happened. *It's because of me.*

She also knew he was not in the mood for answering questions, the matter being a very sensitive one. She kept quiet because she knew him. Asking him about it would be counterproductive. All in all, it had been a lovely night. For the first time in a year, she felt truly happy again.

Anita looked at Emeka and discovered that he had been staring at her.

"Honey, about what happened while we were apart—"

"Shhh!" he cut her off. 'Let's leave the past in the past. Okay?"

"Okay."

"Good. This is a fresh start for both of us, a new beginning, and we have a special blessing that will spice it off. Come, follow me," he said as he stood up and beckoned to his wife.

She followed him downstairs. He opened the door to a room by the left, and they entered. The room was filled with a lot of baby wears. Bob was attending to the baby.

"Thank you, Bob. Can you give us a minute?" Emeka asked.

"No problem, sir. I'm already through," Bob said as his face beamed with a smile. He left the room.

Anita stared around in awe.

"Yes, you can call this room the nursery. Bob has been taking care of the baby." Emeka went to the bed and lifted the baby, who chuckled on seeing him.

"Hello, kiddo," he said as he kissed the baby on both cheeks. "You remember when I told you about him?" he asked Anita.

"Yes," she replied.

He handed the baby over to her. "Today marks a new beginning for us, and we are starting this new phase in our lives with this baby by our side. I know we don't have a child. This child is our special blessing. We are going to raise it up together and give him the very best."

Anita smiled as her gaze fell on the baby.

"I promise you, sweetheart, there will be a lot of sweet blessings waiting for us. I will do my best as a husband and a father. I will not fail us again."

The baby looked so tender and fragile.

"He is so happy, so full of life," she observed.

"Yes," Emeka said.

"Have you given him a name yet?" she asked.

"He will be called Matthew."

"Your father's name. But you have problems with your father. You don't want to consider changing the name?"

"No, I don't have problems with my father. It's my father who has problems with me. He still remains my father."

Anita kissed the baby on his forehead and whispered, "Matthew Junior."

"You got it, sweetheart," Emeka said.

Suddenly, his phone started ringing, the shrill ringtone disturbing the beauty of the moment.

"One moment, honey," he said as he picked the call. "Hello."

"Emeka, it's Doctor Robert," the voice at the other end of the line said.

Emeka became instantly alert. "Good morning, Doctor. I am happy that you called. Perhaps my mother has recovered?"

"Please, Emeka, come to the hospital right now. I will be waiting for you in my office," he said with a tone that reeked of urgency.

The call ended. It took him a moment to gather himself together. He didn't know what to make of the call. *My father is there. Why call me?*

"Honey, what is it about?" Anita asked.

"Sweetheart, please look after of the baby. It's the doctor taking care of my mother. He called and said he wanted to see me there right now. I will be back soon," he said then rushed upstairs, brushed up, and put on fresh clothes.

When he came out of the house, Bob had already started the Cadillac. He smiled as he entered the car. "Head to Rose Hill."

"Yes, sir."

Yusuf opened the gate for them, and Bob drove the car out of the compound.

He avoided my question. What is this about? Emeka wiped off the sweat forming on his forehead as a worried expression clouded his face.

***

They reached the hospital within ten minutes. Emeka entered and was quickly ushered into the doctor's office. He met Dr. Robert pacing uncomfortably around his office.

"Sit down, Emeka. I have been waiting for you."

He had now become familiar with the hospital. The doctor's vast office was crammed with heavy books as usual. He sat down uneasily on a comfortable chair facing the huge desk covered with papers and files and wondered what the whole thing was all about.

The doctor sat down on his seat. "As you told me on the day your mother was admitted into this hospital, you said there was a heated argument between you and her. Suddenly as this was going on, she tumbled and fainted. Am I correct?"

Emeka stiffened. *Where is this going?* He nodded slowly.

It took the doctor a long moment before he spoke again. He knew Emeka was worried. "Emeka, I'm afraid to—"

"What is it, Doctor?" he quickly interrupted.

"We made a startling discovery," the doctor said.

"Enlighten me." His heart was pounding wildly.

"What triggered your mother's heart attack was not the confrontation that went on between you and her that day," Dr. Robert said.

Emeka was now very uncomfortable. "I don't understand, Doctor. What are you saying? You are implying that there is something else?"

"We did a series of tests and found traces of arsenic in her bloodstream and digestive tract," the doctor said.

Emeka sat rooted on his chair as an uncontrollable shiver ran through him.

"What?" He took a few seconds to compose himself. "And what is arsenic?"

"It's a tasteless, dangerous, and deadly poison. Chronic exposure to arsenic even at low levels is associated with an increased risk of cardiovascular disease, coronary heart disease, stroke, and death. Your mother didn't just have a heart attack. She also had jaundice, hypertension, and diarrhoea. Earlier this morning, she told me she has abdominal pain. Whoever did this had been giving her small doses for some months. Your mother is lucky to still be alive."

"Oh my God!"

"Your mother confessed that she smokes. Did you know of that before?" the doctor asked.

"She smokes? My mother? No. I am just hearing about this for the first time," Emeka replied, surprised.

"Smoking makes her susceptible to heart diseases."

"Doctor, what does this all mean?"

Dr. Robert looked at Emeka. "It means that someone very close to your mother, someone who knows her weaknesses, someone who knows everything about her, attempted to kill her. Someone wants your mother dead."

A sick feeling of panic got hold of Emeka. What he heard sent a cold chill up his spine. "Jesus!"

"Yes, it looks bad," the doctor said.

Emeka rested his hands on his head, a thoughtful expression covering his face. "Doctor, why consult with me first? You should have told my father about this. He had been in your hospital with my mother since Monday."

The doctor stared at him for a long time. He didn't want to appear confused. "Ha! I thought you already know. I don't understand this communication gap. It's strange, isn't it?"

Emeka avoided the question. "You thought I knew what?"

"Your father is no longer in the hospital."

That's odd. He maintained an unusual calm. "What happened?"

"You tell me," the doctor said. "He stormed out of the hospital two days ago. From the look on his face as he was leaving the ward, your father was not happy. I don't know what went wrong."

Strange. My father cannot leave his dying wife in the hospital just like that. He is devoted to her.

Emeka sprang up from his seat. "Doctor, how is my mother? Can I see her?"

"She is in a bad shape right now. After your father left, we had to rush in there and put things under control. I don't know what happened. We almost lost her." The doctor wanted to say something else but decided against it. "Alright, don't talk to her or disturb her. You can just go and see her."

Emeka was feeling uneasy.

"Doctor, please do everything possible to save my mother, whatever it takes," he pleaded.

"I will do my best."

They shook hands. Emeka left the office and went straight to his mother's ward. He sat down in a seat close to her bed. She appeared to be in a dreamland with all sorts of I.V.s and drips hooked to her body.

He didn't know whether she was conscious or not. As he sat down observing her, his mind was replaying the doctor's words ...

"We did series of test and found traces of arsenic in her bloodstream and digestive tract. Someone very close to your mother, someone who knows everything about her, attempted to kill her. Someone wants your mother dead."

The doctor's words greatly shook him up like an earthquake. On his way back home, he was greatly distressed.

This is serious. Who will want my mother dead, and why?

CHAPTER TWENTY-SEVEN

"Honey, take it easy. Be careful. Come back soon," Anita said as she hugged her husband.

Bob carried his master's briefcase and put it inside the trunk of the blue Infiniti jeep.

"I will," Emeka promised.

"And you, Bob, you often over-speed. Don't drive too fast," she said to him.

"Yes, Ma," Bob replied.

Immediately after Emeka came back, he had told her everything the doctor had told him. They agreed that he should go to Enugu and tell his father. He would be shocked to hear the news that someone wanted to kill his wife. But he had to know. He might have an idea about who was behind it.

Emeka bid his wife farewell and entered the car. In five minutes' time, they were on their way to Enugu. It was already ten a.m., the weather very bright.

How will my father take this? Will he accuse me of being behind this? Who is this enemy? Her fellow nurses? The maids in her house? Who hates my mother so much that he or she would want her dead?

A lot of unanswered questions troubled his mind. He felt weak and sleepy. As they passed Port-Harcourt-Aba Expressway, he was already in a deep sleep. Bob ignored his madam's order and drove faster. They reached Enugu in the afternoon. He stopped the car in front of the gate and blew the horn. Samuel opened the gate for them.

"Sir."

"Oga!"

Emeka opened his eyes as the sunrays blinded his vision. He was sweating.

"We are here, sir," Bob said.

Emeka nodded and stepped out of the car.

Samuel came forward and greeted him. "Good afternoon, sir."

"Good afternoon, boy. I hope my father is around."

"Yes, he is in the living room."

Emeka nodded and turned to Bob. "Bob, settle down in one of the guest rooms. You need to rest. Good job."

"Thanks, sir."

Emeka walked tiredly into the house. Immediately after he'd opened the door, he found himself staring into the eyes of his father. Father and son stared at each other for a long moment.

"Good afternoon, Papa," Emeka finally managed to say.

His father was sitting down on a sofa, resting.

"You didn't notify me about your visit, son. Anyway, come in and sit down," he said.

Emeka sat down on a sofa facing his father.

"How is your mother doing?" Matthew asked.

"Papa, that's the reason I came to see you."

His father's eyes shifted. He became alert. "What happened?"

"Papa, it's troubling news. I don't know how to put it," he said.

"Just be blunt, son. Don't sugar-coat it."

Emeka nodded. "According to the doctor, it was not the argument I had with her that triggered the heart attack. The doctor said that she was poisoned."

"Hmmm," his father mumbled.

"Papa, our differences aside, this is the time for our family to stand together and fight a common enemy. Someone wants her dead. We need to find out who."

"Hmmm."

What is he thinking? Emeka asked himself as he observed his father. "And Papa, the doctor said you left the hospital abruptly. Why?"

Silence.

After a minute, his father looked at him. "Son, I was the one that poisoned your mother. She had to die, and she will."

Is this a dream?

It took Emeka a minute to make sense of what he'd just heard.

Oh my God! He gasped as his whole body trembled like someone suffering from pneumonia. He couldn't believe it. *My father is the gentlest person I've ever known. He is a man of peace, and he can't hurt a fly. He is a quiet man.*

"Papa! You? Why will you want to kill your own wife, a woman you love so much?"

He stared in shock as the expression on his father's face changed. Suddenly, his father had become a stranger.

"Son, your mother is not who you believe she is, and our family is not what you think it is. Your mother and I, we have been living a lie for more than thirty-five years. You think you know your mother? Beneath that soft exterior is a cold-hearted woman who is willing to do whatever it takes to get what she wants. I became ineffective, a slave in my own house. When I observed her for years and saw the way she was tearing apart everything I suffered so hard to build, I know I had to end it once and for all."

Emeka's body trembled in pain. He began to feel a slight headache. "Father, I don't understand. What are you saying? You and my mother are the perfect couple. You are so devoted to each other. I find this hard to believe."

Mat looked at his son and knew it was time. He had to know. "Son, there is something I want to tell you."

"What is it, Papa?"

"Your mother has been keeping a secret from both of us for a long time."

"What?"

"She thought she was going to die, so she told me on her sick bed. That was why I left the hospital."

"What secret, Father?" Emeka asked.

"It's about your biological father," his father said quickly.

Emeka looked puzzled. "You mean you are not my biological father?"

"Yes. Your mother cheated on me for many years. There was a time I didn't know she had become an unfaithful wife. She manipulated me, and for many years, I believed you were my son," Mat said as he remembered the pain of his wife's betrayal.

"Who is my father?"

"Patrick."

"Your friend, Patrick? The judge?"

"Yes, Patrick is your father."

Emeka's eyes widened.

"That's just the tip of the iceberg. Your mother was not the woman I wanted to marry. I never loved her. I already had a woman I wanted to marry. In fact, I had to cancel the wedding and marry your mother. We were from the same village. My parents threatened they would die an untimely death if I did not marry her. My father threatened to curse me. I was caught between the devil and the blue sea. She was forced down on me by my parents, and she manipulated her way into my heart. I broke the heart of the woman I loved and gave up on her at the eleventh hour. I know she will never forgive me. The decision to marry your mother soon became my greatest regret in life, and it came back to haunt me."

Emeka was speechless. He sat motionless on the sofa.

"I can't pretend anymore. I can't live a lie anymore. That's why I had to end it. For the past three months, I have been putting small doses in her food. I wanted her to suffer what I had suffered and then die in great pain."

"Jesus Christ!" Emeka gasped. "You poisoned her before she told you the truth. You knew about her infidelity before then?"

"Yes, I knew. I am the most patient observer. Your mother was careful of the finest detail, but I later found out. It took me ten years to study your mother and discover that she has been cheating on me. So, when you were ten, I went to the hospital and did a paternity test.

"I was shocked when they told me that we didn't match. You were not my son. At first, I didn't want to confront her with the truth for your sake. I didn't want you to have a divided home. As an educationist, it was what I was preaching against. So I lived in pretence for too long until I didn't know who I was anymore.

"But until she told me recently, I never knew who your real father was. Pat was my best friend. We grew up together and went through the worst together. His involvement in all of this caught me off balance. I never expected it."

Shit! Emeka thought.

"I bided my time and waited patiently for the right time. For the past five years, your mother had been on her worst behaviour. At first, she sacked all the maids helping us in the house, including the gateman, without telling me. When I confronted her, she said they were poking their noses in her private life. As if that were not enough, she cooks only when she likes and often left me to starve

"When I started suffering from arthritis, she would go out in the morning and come back in at midnight. You may not know this about your mother, but she smokes and drinks. She goes to clubs at night. A married woman! And a senior nurse. If I confronted her, she would push my wheelchair and I would fall, and she would call me a useless man."

"Hei! She did all that?" Emeka asked in great surprise. *All this had been going on?*

"Yes. That's why I brought Samuel from the village to be helping me. Your mother has been very wicked to me."

"But you were accusing me of trying to kill her when you knew everything all along."

"Yes, for that I am sorry. Please accept my apology, son. At that time, it was better to comfort you with a lie than to hurt you with the truth. I didn't want you to hate your mother. But now, I am tired of it all. I had to tell you the truth about your mother and our family."

"Father, the woman you would have married, is she alive? Who is she? Where is she?"

"So many questions. Be patient, son. You will know very soon."

Emeka nodded. He stood up, approached his father, and held his hands. "Papa, you were the one struggling to raise me up, and you did. You are the one that had always been in my life. Without you, I wouldn't have been where I am today. Even when there was no money, at the darkest times, you were always there for me. I will never desert you now that you need me the most. You are my father. You will always be my father."

Mat was touched by his son's words. They embraced each other.

"What happened between you and my mother stays between you and her. What happens between me and my wife stays between me and her. We all have our battles and demons to fight. No one else can be able to judge us because they can't understand our pain and they didn't tread our path. My mother must have hurt you so much. She has manipulated us for so long. We now have to pick up the pieces together and stay strong because we are family. Every other thing can break apart, but the bond we share together is stronger than whatever will seek to destroy us."

Emeka wiped his tears, and his father nodded and told him to go and rest. The events of the past week had greatly overwhelmed him. He went to a guest room upstairs and fell into a deep sleep.

CHAPTER TWENTY-EIGHT

Emene, Enugu

The sun was shining, the weather bright—all in all, it was supposed to be a perfect Saturday. But cries and wailings of sorrow shattered the serene atmosphere. The town of Emene would never remain the same again.

Earlier that day, Emeka had briefed his father about Amaka and the baby. Upon hearing about her death, his father had wept bitterly. They'd agreed to travel to Emene and meet with the family.

It took Bob, Emeka, and his father forty minutes to reach the vast town of Emene. As soon as they stepped out of the car, Bob helped Emeka's father to sit on the wheelchair. Within ten minutes, they had joined the small crowd gathered at the Okafor family to condole with them as they paid their final respect to late Amaka Okafor.

They met with the whole family who were dressed in the same uniform. Emeka and his father sat with the bereaved parents in the living room. Mat brought out his white handkerchief and wiped the tears in his eyes. He then took out a fat envelope and handed it over to Amaka's father.

"There will never be another girl like Amaka. I remember when she was with me at Enugu. She was so tender, lovely, and caring. She would always say, 'Papa, go and rest. I will take care of it.' I believed her. She was so hard-working; her death has left a deep hole in our hearts. Please accept our deepest sympathy."

The old man collected the envelope and shook hands with Mat and Emeka.

Mat continued. "We will take care of the baby and give him the best. He remains a living memory of his late mother. As part of our commitment to keep Amaka's name alive, my son and I have agreed to open a foundation in her name. The foundation will be controlled by your family. It will take care of the poor in the society and offer scholarships to bright students especially those from this community. Amaka will forever be alive in our hearts."

The sad faces of Amaka's parents beamed with joy.

"Thank you so much, sir. You have already done enough for our family. We will forever remain grateful," Amaka's father said.

Emeka embraced him and wished them well. Within ten minutes' time, they were already on their way back to Enugu.

***

"Emeka, how is your wife doing? Bob told me she is back in the house," Mat said.

Father and son were in the dining room eating Jollof rice on Sunday evening inside the duplex in Enugu.

Emeka dug his fork into a huge piece of chicken meat and tore it apart with his teeth. "She is doing better now."

"Son, I'm sorry for the way things happened between us over the past five years. Five years ago when you first brought her here, I was rude to you. My parents forced a woman on me, and it was wrong of me to repeat history and try to do the same to you. Then, I always agreed with Rita and her selfish ideas.

Marriage is life. As you live, you make mistakes and learn from them. You made the right decision by finding a good woman that fits you and going ahead to marry her. I apologize for failing you as a father at that time, and I hope she forgives me."

"No, no, no, Father. I am your son. You shouldn't apologize to me. I understand. You didn't fail me as a father; you were there when I needed you the most. It's okay, Dad," Emeka said.

At that moment, the phone he had placed on the dining table began to ring. *My wife?* He picked it up immediately.

"Emeka on the line," he said.

"Emeka, it's Dr. Robert."

He stopped eating and sat upright. "Oh, Doctor, happy Sunday. How is your family?"

He tried to melt down the tension that he felt whenever he was speaking with the doctor. Mat also stopped eating and listened.

"They are fine. Please, Emeka, let me be quick about this. It's urgent. I need you and your father at Rose Hill tomorrow."

"But, Doctor, is there—" Emeka heard the click sound and discovered that the doctor had ended the call.

"What is it about?" Mat asked.

"The doctor said that both of us should meet him at the hospital tomorrow. He said that it's urgent."

"Okay. We will do just that," Mat said.

"I don't like the sound of that," Emeka added.

He had now lost appetite for eating. He wiped his mouth, washed his hands, and thanked his father. He stood up and sauntered to his room.

The doctor was in a haste to end the call. What's going on?

The more he thought of it, the more difficult it proved for him to find the answers.

***

They left Enugu on Monday morning, and in three-and-a-half hours, they were already in Port Harcourt.

"Should we go first to the house?" Bob inquired of his boss.

"No, let's go to the hospital first," Emeka who was sitting close to his father in the backseat, said.

Within twenty minutes, they had already reached the hospital. Bob parked the car at the garage and stepped out.

"You two should go. I will wait in the car," Mat said.

Emeka nodded and stepped out of the car. The two men walked briskly and were soon ushered into the doctor's office. On seeing them, Dr. Robert lifted up his short frame and greeted them with a fixed smile on his face. "Welcome, please sit."

They all sat on the chairs facing the doctor who observed them and asked, "Emeka, what of your father?"

"He is waiting for us in the car. This won't take long, right?"

"No, it won't. Can I get you any drink?"

"No, Doctor. You said it's urgent. What is it about?" Emeka asked.

Dr. Robert brought out a bottled water and filled a glass which he gulped down. "It's about your mother."

Emeka leaned closer, placing his hands on the desk. "How is she doing?"

"Oh, she was a fighter," the doctor said.

That's odd.

"Doctor, I don't want you to be beating around the bush. Be straightforward with me."

Dr. Robert folded his hands together, now wearing a serious expression on his face. "Emeka, I'm sorry. She didn't make it. She gave up last night."

Emeka's blood ran cold. Suddenly, he was looking like a man fighting to get hold of his emotions.

"This is the most difficult part of being a doctor. You asked me to do my best to save her. I did. We cure, God heals. I didn't want her to die. The effects of the poison were too much in her body. It had already destroyed lots of her vital organs. There was nothing much we could do."

Bob flinched in his chair. Emeka stood up and almost fell down. Bob was quick to get hold of his master.

"Show us the body," Emeka said in a trembling voice.

"Alright. Please follow me," the doctor said.

"Doctor, wait," Emeka said. His gaze fell on Bob. "Set my father's wheelchair and help him out of the car. He needs to come with us."

Bob replied with a nod and went out. He helped Emeka's father to get out of the car and onto the wheelchair, and in no time, they were all following the doctor to the morgue.

The doctor opened the door, and they all went in. There was only one bed in the sterile room illuminated only by an electric bulb. A body covered in white sheet lay on the bed. The doctor removed the sheet. Emeka saw the body and almost fainted. Bob covered his mouth with his right hand.

Mother!

Emeka observed her intimidating length. Even in death, she was still a towering figure. He shuddered when he stared at her face. It was completely disfigured.

"The effect of the poison," the doctor said.

A wave of emotions surged through Emeka's body. He knelt down and began to cry. Mat's face remained devoid of any emotion. He stayed silent, watching the whole thing unfold.

The doctor faced Mat. "Sir, I can't begin to imagine the pain your family will go through. This is a great loss. It pains me every time I lose a patient. I asked God why? I feel incompetent and ashamed. Please accept my heartfelt condolence. May her soul rest in peace."

Emeka didn't know what happened next. He felt like he was semi-conscious.

"We will have to bury her quickly. Her body is already rotten," someone was saying.

***

At home, his wife couldn't console him. Knowing that he would never see his mother again made him feel empty, and knowing that the person who had brought about her untimely death was her own husband and his father made the pain even worse.

The irony of life. There'd been times when he'd hated his mother, times he'd been tired of her, but now knowing she was no more, he began to realize how valuable she had been in his life.

The week went by quickly, and on Saturday, a low-key burial ceremony was held at their compound in Emene.

"She was so good to us. Your mother will be greatly missed. May God grant her eternal rest." The Okafor family all said sweet words as they paid their final respect.

At noon, Emeka watched as they began to lower his late mother into the grave dug in front of their house. He was leaning on his wife's shoulder.

Suddenly, a thought entered his mind. The scar! There was a scar on his mother's neck. He hadn't noticed it on the corpse. He rushed to the graveside.

"Please bring up the casket! I want to see my mother! I want to see the corpse!" he was shouting.

But no one was listening. The priest standing closer to him patted him on the shoulder. "Son, I understand that you love her so much you don't want to accept that she's dead. God giveth and He hath taken her away. I know you feel like you want to see her one last time and pay your final respect. I believe she's with God now. You have to let go."

Emeka wasn't listening. He was in a dreamland. Hands were holding him, pushing him back. *You have to let go.*

The words of the priest vibrated in his mind. Mat held the hand of his son. A tear dropped from his eyes as the casket was finally lowered to the ground inside the grave.

Emeka removed the grip of his father and staggered back, almost falling. Tender hands held him now.

"It's alright, honey. You will be fine. I'm here," Anita said.

Emeka was not listening—he was thinking. *Is there something completely wrong with all of this, or am I being paranoid?*

CHAPTER TWENTY-NINE

Benin City
Two months later

Benin, the foothold of the old Benin, was a city where the relics of the old met with its traditions of the present. The Binis, the original natives of the city, were known for sculpture, bronze, its casting skills, and their arts and crafts. The old city with its famous culture and artefacts was home to one of the oldest sustained monarchies in the world.

Decades ago, its fixation with its cultural history and its focus on the achievements of the past had made it to be a city fixed in just one place in time. Today, Benin had evolved into a city bustling with commercial activity that could only be rivalled by its rich cultural heritage. With its priceless cultural artefacts and urbanized environs, Benin, the capital of Edo state and the centre of the Bini kingdom, was much alive in its over-three-thousand-year-old history that defined its past and its present.

At the centre of the city, inside a two-storey residential villa located in Ehaekpen Street, two long-time friends stood up from opposite sides of the huge living room, approached each other at the centre, and embraced tightly.

The two women, both at sixty-five years of age, had each played the part of 'friend' and 'enemy' alike in the over fifty years they had known each other. They had both the gut and the steel. With so much in common, their determination to make and mar had both created and destroyed, shaping their lives and that of their loved ones in ways they would never comprehend.

The second woman was sobbing silently, getting ready to break down again in tears. Today was her final day in Benin. After hiding in her friend's house for two months, she was finally ready to go home. A huge dog, a third occupant in the house, stood up from where it was sitting down in the room and ran to her, licking her legs and shaking its tail.

"It's alright, Bomber. I will miss you so much," the woman said as she bent down and caressed the soft hairs of the dog's body.

She stood up and faced the first woman. "Thank you, Emilia. Your hospitality is unmatched," she said as she kept sobbing.

"Stop crying, my dear. You must not give up now. You have not lost them," Emilia, the first woman and the host, said.

As a female lawyer, she was the ultimate success story. A woman who didn't just mingle with the top politicians and the top one percent, she was a bigwig herself. They always came to her for help. Over the past two decades, she had become a lawyer who worked for the highest bidders, defending the guilty, the corrupt, and the shameless.

Her clients' list ranged from the multinational corporations in the Niger delta whose activities destroyed people's lands and rivers, to corrupt governors who rigged elections and appeared in court every month as they paid any amount necessary just to fight for their survival and remain on the seat of power, to guilty elites that got away with almost everything.

Emilia was one of the few female lawyers who had climbed to the top of the ladder in their career, a feat she'd accomplished ten years ago when she became a Senior Advocate of Nigeria. A bulldog both in the court room and outside of its walls, she had almost everything she wanted.

She had only one regret. She'd chased love at an early age and married on time, but then had turned her back on love and married her career. As a consequence, even as old age beckoned, she had no child of her own. Since she'd divorced and parted ways with her husband one year into her marriage, she had said no to long-term commitment, men, and marriage. Emilia had always been a true feminist. Today, she was a role model to young independent women.

Emilia was six feet tall, dark, and had the appearance that whispered 'Mighty woman.' A stubborn observer of her physical appearance would swear that she was once a beautiful girl in her prime. Now, she had strong features that resisted the temptations of old age and had a vegetarian diet to back it up.

She was dressed in a red designer gown covered with a diamond necklace that cost a fortune. Her automated two-storey mansion was a house that screamed 'wonders,' the best that money could provide. Everything in the house was voice and device-controlled. The expensive Picasso paintings on the walls had been given to her by a former First Lady, her closest friend. The ground tiles were as transparent as the LCD screen that covered the walls of the living room.

"I know, Emilia. I am afraid of losing them. If I lose them, I have lost everything," the second woman, Rita Obi, said. She sat down on an enormous chair that smelt of new money as she held Bomber with tender hands.

"Let me prepare food for you. You need to eat before you go," Emilia said.

"Thank you, Emilia."

Emilia nodded. "Door open."

A glass door opened, and she left and proceeded to the kitchen.

Rita Obi closed her eyes in tears as a two-month old memory resurfaced in her mind; a reminder of how she'd escaped an almost inevitable fate.

***

Two Months Earlier
Rose Hill Hospital, Port Harcourt

Two month ago, Rita was in Rose Hill Hospital, staring death in the face while fighting for her life. When she'd finally opened her eyes, she had seen her husband by her bedside.

"Mat, is that you?" she had asked. Her vision had still been blurred.

"Yes, my dear, it's me."

"You are here. You came."

She could see clearly now. She felt so happy when she realized that her husband was with her by her bedside. To rid herself of the source of her nightmares and come clean in front of him, she told him her well-kept secret, and in a sudden turn of events, he got angry and stormed out of the hospital.

She'd panicked when he stared at her, something odd and terrifying about the expression on his face. She had never seen that look on his face before. Her husband appeared dangerous, like a vengeful angel sent from the pit of Hell to take her back to the land of the dead.

She shivered and almost lost her life in the process. For more than one hour, the doctor and his nurses stayed by her side and were able to stabilize her. "I will die. I will die," was all she was saying.

"Don't panic. I will do anything to save you. You will not die."

The doctor's words gave her hope. In the evening of that day, the doctor told her something that shocked her and brought back all her fears. He did several tests and found traces of arsenic inside her body—in her bloodstream, her digestive track, everywhere.

"I was poisoned?' She almost relapsed into unconsciousness again.

"You whore, you will die here alone. I will go now and get ready for your funeral."

Her husband's words and the deadly expression on his face confirmed her fears that there was someone very close to her that had already tried to kill her.

My son hates me, and my husband detests me. One of them hates me enough to want me dead.

On Thursday, when her son visited her, she was conscious but pretended she didn't feel his presence. Immediately after he left, she quickly requested for the doctor. When Dr. Robert entered her ward, she started speaking as much words as she could. Dr. Robert listened as his eyes widened.

"To fake your death? That is crazy. I could lose my license. You want me to deceive your family and lie to everyone. It's against the principles of my profession."

"Doctor, please," Rita said. "You're an intelligent man. You have been taking care of me for the past five days. You know that something is deeply wrong. You detected the poison in my system. You know that someone wants me dead. It's against your principle? Is that what you are saying? I am a nurse. What is against the principles of your profession is leaving me here to die when you know what to do to save my life. You swore a special oath to save the lives of your patients.

"Please, Doctor. Whoever tried to kill me will try again if he discovers that I am still alive. Let's make the killer believe that he has succeeded; let's make him believe that he won. I will pay you three million naira. Help me, please. Save me!"

Her words touched the doctor. Dr. Robert sat down as conflicting thoughts flooded his mind. *"Doctor, please do everything possible to save my mother, whatever it takes."*

Three million naira?

As he thought about his dilemma, he felt pity for his patient even as her son's words vibrated in his mind.

Five minutes later, Rita gasped in great pain as she smiled when the doctor agreed with her plan. For the next three days, the doctor administered her lots of medications that helped to flush out the poison from her system. Everything was top-secret, just between the doctor and his patient.

On Sunday morning, Dr. Robert worked frantically to get a corpse ready. The face was disfigured, and it resembled the physical build and appearance of his patient. When he was ready, Rita told him to call her son and her husband. The whole plan would work only if they would believe the corpse was hers.

Luckily for her, when they came to the hospital on Monday, heard the news of her death, and saw the corpse, they didn't raise any suspicion. Few days later when the doctor told her that the corpse had been laid to rest and she was considered dead and buried, Rita knew she was ready to disappear. She could walk now.

The doctor gave her some drugs, and she hugged him. She quickly did an online money transfer, and the amount was transferred to the doctor's account. She called Emilia afterwards and told her that her life was in danger and she needed to stay with her for a while. Emilia had easily agreed and urged her to start her journey. Three hours later, she was on her way to Benin.

For the past two months, she had been able to regain her strength at her friend's place. She had told Emilia some parts of her story, and Emilia had sympathy for her plight. Now Rita was ready to go back home. But even as she stared at the glass walls and held the dog close to her chest, she didn't know what tomorrow would bring.

CHAPTER THIRTY

Benin

Five minutes later, the glass door opened, and Emilia entered the living room carrying a plate of fried rice and salad. She proceeded to the dining room and set it carefully on the table, her face filled with a smile.

"Food is ready, my dear," she said to Rita.

Rita stood up and went to the dining table. Bomber followed her.

"Thank you," she said as she sat down.

"Don't mention," Emilia whispered and walked out.

The door opened, and she left the room and entered the kitchen. *Now I will wait. In the next ten minutes, Rita will be dead*, she thought as a devilish smile crept to her face.

Emilia's perfect success story was not as perfect as it appeared. Beneath the rich façade of it all lay a unique failure that stared at her in the face every time she thought about her life. Her eyes bore only promises of vengeance, and she had been preparing, getting ready for the day she would finally get rid of the source of her failure and the only reason why she had never been a happy woman.

Emilia had been waiting for this opportunity for a long time until it suddenly landed on her lap. Her arch-enemy and the source of all her bitterness, Rita Obi, had destroyed her marriage twice, snatching both her men away from her. She had been waiting for the day she would pay her back; an eye for an eye. She stared at the walls as she remembered how her wedding day—the happiest day in a woman's life—had turned out to be the worst day in her life.

Forty years ago, young Emilia, then twenty-five years of age, was young, fresh, and full of life. It was a Saturday morning, her wedding day. Her friends were frantically getting her ready for the grand occasion. The makeup artistes, the girls arranging her hair, her beauticians, and her bridesmaids all giggled with her in her father's house at Enugu, getting her ready for the big occasion.

Her eyes were filled with love, anxiousness, and anticipation as she checked the time; eight a.m. She had been waiting for her fiancé, Matthew Obi, who was then a teacher in a secondary school. He was young and educated and had a promising future.

Suddenly, her friends started shouting, "Your King is here!"

They were all happy. Emilia looked up and saw Mat and was surprised. "Why are you not dressed in your wedding suit? There is no time."

She was worried. Mat appeared tense, like someone who had been under a lot of pressure. His clothes were ruffled, and he seemed very tired.

"Honey, can you come out? I want to talk to you briefly."

Emilia was now very worried. She sensed that something was wrong. She nodded reluctantly and came out of the house.

Mat held her hand. "Emilia, I want you to know that I will always love you. You are my first love, you will always be in my heart no matter what happens."

She began to panic. "I know. What is going on, Mat?"

"I am sorry, Emilia. I don't know how to tell you this. I have been awake throughout last night. I couldn't sleep."

She used her hands to cover her eyes; she knew about his parents. They didn't support their son marrying her. He had finally bowed down to their pressure.

"My parents threatened to die if I go ahead with this wedding. I am sorry, Emilia. The wedding has been cancelled. I wish you all the best," Mat was saying.

Emilia was no longer listening. An uncontrollable sob tore out from her throat. The humiliation was too much.

Mat left hurriedly. The next Saturday, Emilia was shocked when she heard that he had wedded Rita, her bitter rival. She heard that both Rita and Mat were from the same town of Emene. Mat's parents considered Emilia to be an outsider and felt that Rita was more suitable for their son. Emilia felt like Rita had snatched her man away from her.

She spent the next couple of weeks crying. The pain and heartbreak she endured were too much to bear. Towards the end of that year, she got admission to study law at University of Nigeria, Enugu Campus. She put her past behind her and moved on.

Four years later, she had fallen in love with Patrick Udo, a lawyer who swept her off her feet. Patrick was brilliant, gentle, and handsome. Emilia told him all about herself. They shared the same interests—she was going to be a lawyer, too.

Six months later, they wedded happily at a small church in New Haven, Enugu. It was a marriage made in Heaven. As fate would have it, Pat was Matthew's friend. Both families were living close to each other in

Enugu. Emilia didn't like the closeness but tried as much as possible to stay away from Rita.

She soon graduated from law school and started working in a law firm. It kept her busy throughout the week. Nine months into her marriage, she arrived home one afternoon and gasped as she struggled to catch her breath. She caught her husband with Rita on their matrimonial bed. She almost fainted.

Rita again! Rita had been married for four years and hadn't given birth. When Rita came to her house and boldly announced that she was pregnant, she knew it was not a coincidence. *My enemy bearing the child of my husband. I won't take it anymore.*

The marriage ended in the bitter divorce that left Emilia in a psychological mess. It took her many months to recover and get back on her feet.

After the divorce, she felt she could no longer stay in Enugu; she said no to men. They were heartbreakers, all the same, she thought. She relocated to Benin and channelled all her bitterness and failures in marriage into a fierce determination that helped her to rise in her legal profession.

Throughout the next thirty-five years, she had always nurtured a deep hatred for Rita and for all she'd done to her. Every time she looked at other women and remembered that she had no child of her own, she felt empty and hated Rita even more.

Now she will die. This is the perfect murder! She had put a very potent rat poison in her food. *It would kill her within seconds. She had already died and had been buried by her family. I am merely saving them from another heartbreak.*

***

Port Harcourt

"Honey, what are you waiting for? We are late for the fundraising," Anita said as the sound of her high heels echoed around the compound.

She stared at Yusuf, and he quickly opened the gate. Bob pressed the button on the remote, and the door of the red Lamborghini opened. He reversed the car slowly and stopped near Anita.

The door of the house opened, and Emeka walked out with a smile on his face. He was fully dressed in a black London suit, looking fresh, powerful, and very much alive. He approached his wife and kissed her briefly on her lips.

Instantly, his phone started to ring. "Please excuse me," he said as he brought out the phone from his pocket and picked the call.

"Emeka," the voice at the other end of the line said.

"Father."

"Son, some months ago, you asked me about the woman that I loved, the woman that I wanted to marry but later cancelled the wedding at the last minute."

Emeka remembered. "Yes. Who is she?"

"Her name is Emilia. She is now a highly successful lawyer residing in Benin." His father's voice was deep. "I know she had never forgiven me and your mother," his father continued. "I don't know exactly when her friendship with your mother started, but after our wedding, your mother being a manipulator with a certificate became her best friend ever since. I know she still nurtures the spirit of revenge. She later got married to another man but got divorced barely a year into the marriage."

"Divorced?" Emeka asked. "Who was her husband?"

"Patrick, your biological father."

Emeka raised his eyebrows. "Patrick? What led to their divorce?"

"Emilia discovered that her husband was cheating on her. She found out even before me about your mum and Pat. It really pained her. It made her relocate to Benin."

This gets worse, Emeka thought.

"When she found out, she called for a divorce. But when you found out that your wife was cheating on you, you didn't want to divorce her," Emeka said.

"Yes. It may have been easy for Emilia because there was no child in her marriage. But in my own marriage, there was a child involved. Even if divorce would be easier for the couples in the marriage, it is always very difficult for the child caught in the middle of its sandstorm. Some end up not having any home. Abandoned by both parents, they wind up being switched from one orphanage home to another. They would never know love. Some pass through traumatic childhood experiences. I didn't want that kind of life for you. I had to follow the most difficult pathway. I just wanted to tell you so that you will know about your past, so that you will understand and learn from them."

"Thanks, Dad," Emeka said, and the call ended.

My father, my biological father, my mother, and this Emilia, what a quadruple! Emeka thought as he followed his wife and entered the car. He sat down, held his wife, and started composing his speech in his mind, unaware of what was going on hundreds of miles away.

***

Benin

Emilia changed the expression on her face, and her well-crafted smile appeared back. The door opened, and she entered the living room and started walking confidently to the dining room.

Suddenly, she stopped in her tracks. She almost shouted in panic as she covered her mouth with her right hand. Her only friend and companion, her dog, Bomber lay dead on the floor, and Rita was sitting down, staring at her, giving her a mocking smile.

"Nkechi!" Rita called her name as she flashed her sparkling white teeth.

"Ada," Emilia said as she called her friend's name, wondering why she was still alive, her eyes filled with surprise.

CHAPTER THIRTY-ONE

Benin

Ada, whose other name was also Rita, said to her friend, "You know, when everyone wants you dead, you have to start thinking ten steps ahead. You have to be very conscious and smart. Sometimes, you need to beat someone at their own game by making them believe they had won."

She paused for a moment then continued, "But Nkechi, why? I thought you have forgiven me? I have spent all those years making up for all that I had done. We had become best friends."

"Best friends, my foot!" Nkechi, whose other name was Emilia, cut in. "Ada, there are things you don't understand. There are natural laws that order the universe and the actions of people. No matter how far you run, Ada, you can never run away from your past. They will always catch up with you."

Ada laughed for a long time. "You didn't know this, law expert. I normally feed the dog before I eat. I have always done it since the very first day I came to your house. I am very kind, wasn't I? When I gave the dog a little bite of the rice and it dropped down dead a few minutes later, I wasn't surprised. This time, it took you long to serve the food. I never underestimated you, Emilia. You have always been a stubborn enemy, a caring friend, and a formidable foe.

"Now let me make this simple. Today is the day we plan to say goodbye, and that is what will happen. I can report you to the police for attempting to kill me, or I can just walk away and forget that this ever happened. You know you can be charged for attempted murder; it will damage your reputation. You will be disbarred. And it will destroy the little that is left of your miserable life. Your choice."

Emilia smiled and nodded. Quickly, she put her hand under the huge chair beside her and brought out a gun. Rita's eyes widened.

"And I always have a Plan B for everything. You are mistaken, Rita. The fact is that everybody believes you are dead. It is better for that fact to remain unchanged. And you know what? Your family is ready to deny that you are still alive. Your so-called husband will swear that you have died long ago. So you see, your second death will not raise any suspicions. It is you being alive here at every minute that will raise suspicions."

Suddenly, both women stared at each other, and in the briefest seconds, fear registered in Rita's eyes.

Emilia and Rita's 'frenemy' relationship went back all the way to their secondary school days. Rita remembered how Emilia had snatched her first love from her. She was pregnant for the guy then and barely fifteen, young and innocent. But experience changed people. The guy, Peter, had denied being responsible for the pregnancy to the school authorities. The school had expelled Rita, and to avoid the shame she would bring to her family, she had terminated the pregnancy and entered another school.

She felt less a woman, lived in shame and 'had I knowns.' She later heard that Peter had quickly dumped Emilia for another girl. He had played them both, turning them against each other and causing them to treat men with a unique disdain later in their lives. She had sworn that time that Emilia would pay for what she had done to her.

For the next few years, fate brought them together. Rita had always sought to impress people in her village. Her family resided close to where Mat's parents were living. She didn't know the couple were fond of her until when their son wanted to marry. She didn't know Mat was already planning to marry Emilia, a girl he'd met in the city.

She found out from Mat's parents on the eve of her wedding day. When she discovered that Mat had cancelled his wedding with Emilia and agreed to marry her, she had been overjoyed; it was the happiest day in her life.

She had never loved Mat, feeling he was too gentle and too nice. She had always dreamt of marrying a real man. Her impression of Mat was that he was just a teacher with no mind of his own. The marriage was more of an arrangement between the two families.

Two years into the marriage, Rita, then a final-year nursing student, had already grown bored of it all. Four years into the marriage, no child yet. Then, Emilia had gotten married to Patrick, a young, charming lawyer. Patrick was her husband's best friend, and both families were living in the same city, close to each other.

The first time Rita set her eyes on Patrick, she felt butterflies in her stomach. After some time, she began to think about him a lot. Whenever she saw him, her heart would start beating faster. Pat was the kind of man she wanted. Rita was already frustrated in her marriage. Her husband was always busy. Every night, he would come back late, very tired.

Emilia, then, was a fresh law graduate working in a law firm, and Rita was a graduate nurse looking for a job in a government hospital. When she was not out looking for a job, she was in the house feeling lonely and bored.

Patrick was always coming to Rita's house to visit her husband. Earlier that year, Rita and her husband had gone for fertility tests to know the cause of their infertility. When she had found out from the result of the test that her husband was not fertile, she'd almost lost hope of having a child. When she saw Pat for the first time, he'd ignited in her an unquenchable passion. Suddenly, she had become a lonely housewife in need of a man, and a desperate woman in need of a child.

Anxious to have a baby of her own, Rita knew what she had to do when a wonderful opportunity presented itself. She began the perfect seduction of Patrick. All it took was for Pat to lose control for the first time in his life and give in to the temptation of a beautiful, lonely woman, a seductress willing to go to any length to get what she wanted.

They started the affair that got her pregnant and cost Patrick his marriage. Her busy husband believed it was his, and Rita soon gave birth to a son they happily named Emeka.

But only a woman knows the father of her child. Emilia was quick to find out about her cheating husband and Rita, and it pained her so much. When their marriage ended in bitter divorce, Emilia left the city as Rita was nursing her baby.

Years later, Rita sought to cultivate a new friendship with Emilia. They became the best of friends even when they secretly hated each other. Now, the cat was out of the bag, pitting two bitter enemies once again against each other.

***

Rita stared at the gun pointed at her and fidgeted. But she'd expected it.

"And I have my own Plan B. For over two months, I have been the most patient observer." She was staring into the eyes of Emilia now. "I discovered that there are three things you love so much in your life. You can't do without them. The first is your dog which is already dead. The second is this house that everyone stares at in wonder. Pictures of this house are in lots of magazines with everyone discussing its worth.

"But the truth is that it's actually a fortress. Deep inside you, you are still a weak little girl. You stay here and hide from the rest of the world. The third is yourself; you love yourself so much. I have already paid the most dangerous gang in this city a lot of money to burn down this house to the ground if they call me in the next ten minutes and I don't pick the call. Go ahead. Call my bluff and shoot me."

Rita now had a deadly glare in her eyes. Emilia was startled by what Rita had just told her.

"You are bluffing. What you don't know is that a lot of people have already tried to burgle and destroy this house. Any attack on this house automatically sets off an alarm located at the building of the divisional police headquarters here in this city."

"Ha ha ha," Rita laughed. "The Police, hmmm. My men don't know that, and they don't need to know. By the time the police come here, you are already dead. You don't know if my men are in the next building already waiting. They have a lot of equipment that will shake the foundation of this house and bring everything to the ground."

Emilia kept quiet, thinking. Rita looked at her watch.

"If they call you, you must pick the call, or I will shoot you," Emilia said.

"I have nothing to lose. Like you said, I have already died. I am ready to die. Shoot me. But I care about you, Emilia. I don't want you to die. So I won't pick the call, and if they hear your voice, they will go ahead with the plan. And you have a lot to lose. You don't want to die now, do you? Your choice."

Emilia was still pointing the gun at her.

Rita looked at her watch. "Five minutes more. My bag is already here. You can kill me and set up a chain of events that will bring about your own destruction, or you can leave me and we take it like we never met. I am leaving now."

Rita walked past her friend, collected her bag, and started walking towards the elevator.

Emilia hissed and lowered the gun. "Stay away from me. Stay the hell away from my life."

"Goodbye," Rita said as she entered the elevator that would take her to the lower floor.

On reaching the ground level, she stepped out of the elevator and walked to the huge gate. The gate opened, and she walked out.

I need a second chance with my family. I have failed as a mother and a wife. It's now that I know I have everything to lose. I need to set things right.

Rita Obi was ready to head back home.

CHAPTER THIRTY-TWO

Port Harcourt
Emeka stared at the wall of his living room as he began to get more worried with every passing minute. That Tuesday evening, Anita was not back yet. Two days earlier when they'd come back from the fundraising ceremony for the Amaka Okafor Foundation located in Enugu, she had started complaining about her health. She was not feeling fine, and she had missed her period.

He had called Dr. Robert who'd said it could be due to a number of reasons. He insisted he would not say anything more until he had seen her. Today, she'd gone to the hospital. Now he was a feeling too impatient as a lot of thoughts kept crossing his mind. He waited and waited until he sat on the chair and slept off.

A blaring car horn woke him up. He quickly rushed down the stairs and met his wife as she was coming out of the car.

"Good evening, sir," Bob greeted, but Emeka didn't reply.

Anita rushed and hugged her husband for a long moment. Emeka breathed a sigh of relief at seeing her.

She gaze at his face, feeling so excited. "Honey, I did the test."

Emeka was anxious now, his heart pounding. "And?"

"Honey, I'm pregnant!"

"Really?"

"Yes."

Is this a dream?

At first, he couldn't believe it, but when the realization that he was going to be a father again crept up to his face, he was overjoyed. He forgot his manners as he jumped up and down in jubilation and then carried his wife in his arms and rushed into the house.

"This calls for celebration, sweetheart. Thank God. Finally," he was saying.

Anita was lying next to her husband on the bed. "Yes, thank God. We believed in each other, stayed strong, and it happened for us."

"Yes, honey. I love you," he whispered in her ear.

"You are the best. I love you, too."

***

The next day, Emeka took his family to Enugu to meet his father. Bob drove the Cadillac while Anita carried Matthew Junior in her arms. Matthew Senior, now aging gracefully, was so happy to see them.

"Welcome, my daughter-in-law."

"Thank you, Papa, "Anita replied as she felt a feeling of déjà vu.

Six years ago, she had come to this house then as a fiancée of their golden son, uncertain of how things would unfold. Today, a lot of things had changed. They ate and chatted and laughed. *This is how it is supposed to be.*

Now, they were all seated in the living room. Matthew cleared his throat and said as he faced Anita, "My daughter-in-law. I am sorry for how our family treated you. It was wrong of us. We are all family, and you are a vital part of us. Emeka told me you are pregnant with his child. I am so happy. I ask for your forgiveness. Please forgive me, Nne."

Anita felt like crying. Emeka held her in his arms.

"Papa, you are like a father to me. I didn't fault you for what happened. Every father must fight for his child to be in the right path. I have forgiven you. You don't have to worry," she said. She stood up and hugged him.

Suddenly, there was a knock on the gate.

"Papa, are we expecting anyone?" Emeka asked.

"No," his father quickly replied.

They remained silent. The gate opened and closed. They heard the sound of someone's footstep. They didn't hear any voice.

Instantly, the door opened, and a figure staggered into the living room. They saw it and immediately rushed to each other, their eyes filled with icy terror, like the people who had seen a ghost. Father, son, daughter-in-law, and driver were all holding onto each other tightly in panic.

This can't be, Matthew thought as he shivered.

Oh my God! Emeka gasped as his wife held him tightly.

"My daughter Anita, Emeka my son, my lovely husband, it's me," Rita Obi said as she stood at the centre of the room like the prodigal child with tears in her eyes.

EPILOGUE

Trans-Ekulu, Enugu
One year later

The rays of the sun had caused the Sunday afternoon to be sunny. Thunder and lightning struck at a far distance. Weather analysts had earlier predicted that rain would fall this Sunday afternoon despite the sunshine, but the Obi family didn't care. All of them were in Enugu spending time in the compound with the two kids, Emeka Junior and Matthew Junior. A celebration of life, they called it.

It had taken them months to reconcile their differences. It hadn't been long since Mat had accepted his wife Rita back. She'd finally confessed that she was suffering from the side effects of the poisoning. The doctor had told her she would develop certain complications later in life. The poisoning had damaged some of her vital organs and had shortened her lifespan. Rita was now a woman still hanging on with the help of the little thread of her life that threatened to cut with each new day. Patrick was also with them.

"Son," Pat said to Emeka. "You know you can always come to my house and pay an old man a visit."

Emeka nodded, and both men hugged each other briefly. His business was doing well now, and he had started initiating moves to take back control of his company.

Anita was with her father-in-law, carrying Matthew Junior. She laughed at something he said as she handed the baby boy to him.

"Big boy," Mat said as he carried the baby. He was so happy. Anita looked up ahead and saw Rita, her mother-in-law, carrying Emeka Junior. Rita was a woman that inspired a lot of things in her.

"I am so sorry, my daughter. I was so focused on the present that I didn't know what tomorrow would bring. I have changed. A near-death experience can melt the most hardened heart. Perhaps I had to go through a near-death experience to be able to come back to my senses. I have been so unkind to you. I know forgiveness is a process. Please may God give you the strength to forgive me," Rita had told her one year ago, the day she'd stumbled into the house like a ghost.

Rita's gaze fell on Anita. Anita waved at her, and Rita smiled. Feeling happy but not knowing what actually caused a change in her mood, Anita went and joined her husband.

"Honey, how are you doing?" Emeka asked.

"Lovely, and you?"

"I am doing so great, sweetheart," he said as he kissed her briefly on her lips.

Emeka looked at the various faces in the compound and smiled. It looked like the picture of the perfect family. Love shone in the eyes of everyone.

As twisted as we are, we are still a family. It is always easier to destroy things that took us a long time to build but more difficult to put the pieces together and build them back. In life, we make mistakes. We learn from them, and we learn to forgive no matter how long it would take us. In life, we learn to give up when there is nothing else to fight for, but we also learn to mend fences and stay together when we know that there is a lot at stake.

He remembered what his father had once told him. "Family is more than just blood. If you lose the bond of family, you have lost everything."

He believed it. As he watched the faces of his loved ones, he knew in his heart that family was everything.

THE END

Thank you for reading Twisted.
If you enjoyed this story, please leave a review.

ABOUT THE AUTHOR

Stanley Umezulike was born and raised in Nigeria. He writes African romance stories, family drama novels and thrillers set in tropical Africa. He is a graduate of Political Science from the University of Nigeria, Nsukka. He found his passion for writing at the age of 14 and he's been writing ever since. He lives in Enugu, Nigeria. Apart from reading and writing, he enjoys watching thriller TV shows, listening to good music and travelling.

Social Media links:

Twitter: https://mobile.twitter.com/stanumezulike
Instagram: https://www.instagram.com/stanley_umezulike/
Facebook: https://www.facebook.com/OfficialStanleyUmezulike1/

OTHER BOOKS BY LOVE AFRICA PRESS

Love at First Sound by Amaka Azie
Diary of a Wallflower by Glory Abah
His Inherited Princess by Empi Baryeh
Ere's Secret & 223 Bonny Street by Firi Kamson
Bound to Liberty by Kiru Taye/Kai Tyler

CONNECT WITH US
Facebook.com/LoveAfricaPress
Twitter.com/LoveAfricaPress
Instagram.com/LoveAfricaPress

www.loveafricapress.com

www.ingramcontent.com/pod-product-compliance
Lightning Source LLC
Chambersburg PA
CBHW021436080526
44588CB00009B/550